W9-BQJ-061

WITHDRAWN

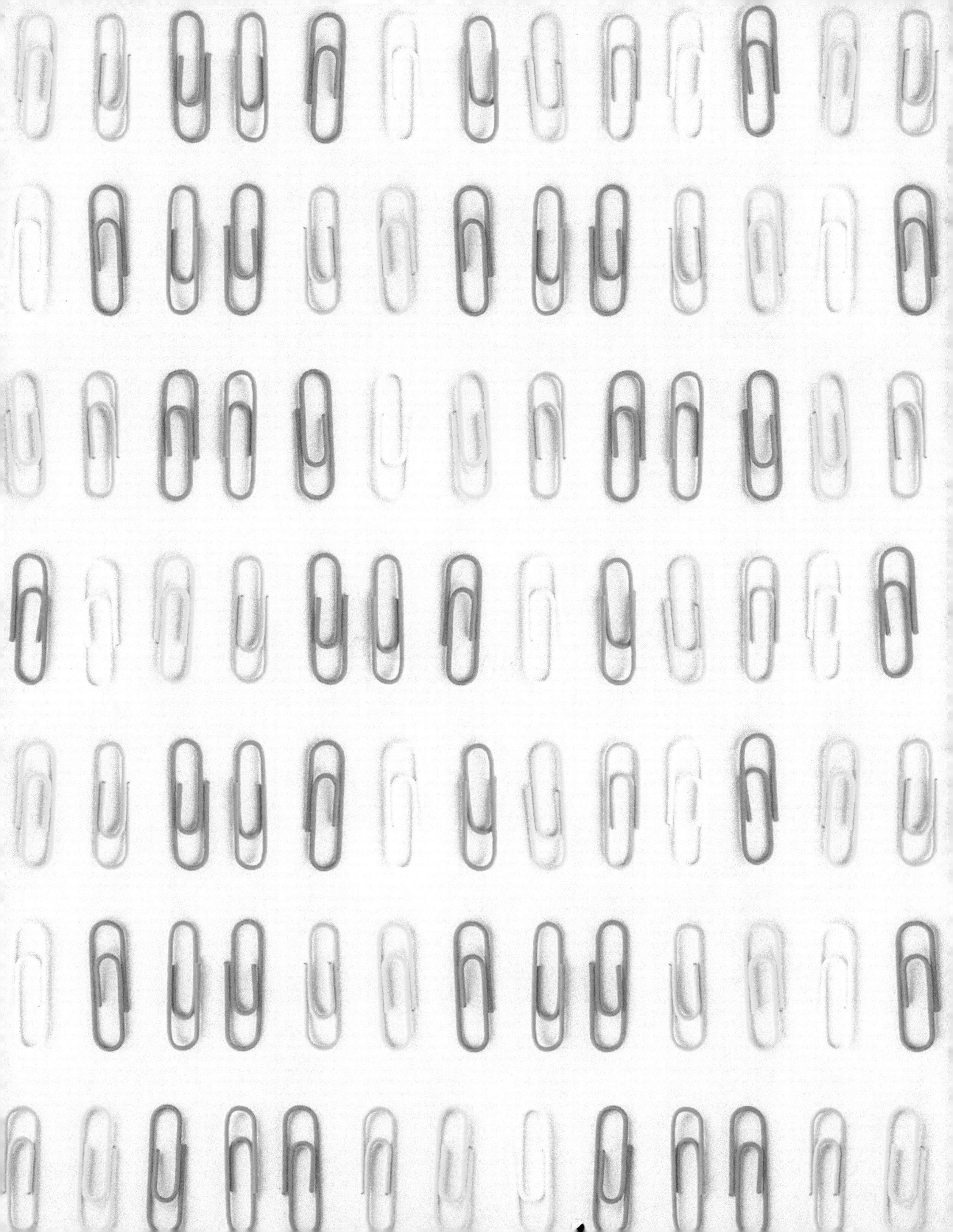

The A+ Homeschool Planner

Plan, Record & Celebrate Each Child's Progress

AMY SHARONY

ROCKRIDGE PRESS

Copyright © 2018 by Rockridge Press, Emeryville, California

No part of this publication may be reproduced, stored in a retrieval system or transmitted in any form or by any means, electronic, mechanical, photocopying, recording, scanning or otherwise, except as permitted under Sections 107 or 108 of the 1976 United States Copyright Act, without the prior written permission of the Publisher. Requests to the Publisher for permission should be addressed to the Permissions Department, Rockridge Press, 6005 Shellmound Street, Suite 175, Emeryville CA 94608.

Limit of Liability/Disclaimer of Warranty: The Publisher and the author make no representations or warranties with respect to the accuracy or completeness of the contents of this work and specifically disclaim all warranties, including without limitation warranties of fitness for a particular purpose. No warranty may be created or extended by sales or promotional materials. The advice and strategies contained herein may not be suitable for every situation. This work is sold with the understanding that the Publisher is not engaged in rendering medical, legal or other professional advice or services. If professional assistance is required, the services of a competent professional person should be sought. Neither the Publisher nor the author shall be liable for damages arising herefrom. The fact that an individual, organization or website is referred to in this work as a citation and/or potential source of further information does not mean that the author or the Publisher endorses the information the individual, organization or website may provide or recommendations they/it may make. Further, readers should be aware that Internet websites listed in this work may have changed or disappeared between when this work was written and when it is read.

For general information on our other products and services or to obtain technical support, please contact our Customer Care Department within the U.S. at (866) 744-2665, or outside the U.S. at (510) 253-0500.

Rockridge Press publishes its books in a variety of electronic and print formats. Some content that appears in print may not be available in electronic books, and vice versa.

TRADEMARKS: Rockridge Press and the Rockridge Press logo are trademarks or registered trademarks of Callisto Media Inc. and/or its affiliates, in the United States and other countries, and may not be used without written permission. All other trademarks are the property of their respective owners. Rockridge Press is not associated with any product or vendor mentioned in this book.

Photography © KucherAV/Shutterstock.com, cover, p.2; Maglara/Shutterstock.com, cover, p.1.

Author Photograph © JES Photography 2018

ISBN: Print 978-1-64152-081-2

Contents

How to Use This Planner

Like any great adventure, homeschooling goes a little more smoothly when you have a good map to help you find your way. That's the purpose of this planner—to help you figure out, step by step, what a great homeschool year looks like for your family and to plot a course to get there, one year, one month, one week, one day at a time.

Think of this planner as your own personal homeschool support network. Yes, you can count on it to help you keep track of your everyday routine, but it's also designed to help you stay focused on your family's bigger homeschool goals. What kind of educational experience do you want your children to have? How do you want your homeschool to feel? On that day when your kids finish their homeschool careers and head off on their next big life adventures, what do you want them to think about their homeschool experience? These questions are just as important as deciding what math curriculum to use.

Some people start with a mission statement—a big-picture goal for their homeschool. (*I want my children to grow up in a supportive, caring space that teaches them how to learn,* or *Our homeschool will academically and emotionally prepare our children for college and careers.*) Others start with specifics: *Our homeschool will be grounded in literature,* or *We will integrate STEAM into all of our learning,* or *I want to create an environment where student-led learning can thrive.* Some people are more visual and prefer to focus on creating a mood board or a Pinterest board that captures the spirit they want for their homeschool. There's no one right way to homeschool, and there's no one right way to set goals for your homeschool. Your right way is always the way that works best for your family, and it may take a little trial and error to figure that out. That's just part of the process.

This planner is part of the process, too. Use it the way that works for your homeschool. Do you like to schedule every minute and activity? You'll find tons of space to schedule multiple subjects for up to six students. Is your homeschool more of a plan-as-you-go laboratory? The space works equally well as a journal to track your day-by-day activities. Get deep into details or stick to basics—whatever your planning style, this planner will help you manage your homeschool life with confidence. I've also included some of the best tips for homeschooling I've collected over my decade as a homeschool mom (and the editor of a homeschool magazine)—these are some of the homeschooling life lessons I wish someone had clued me into back when we first started homeschooling—and some of my favorite learning-related quotations to inspire you along the way.

Let's get started! Pour yourself a cup of coffee, grab your favorite pen, and get ready to explore your planner one section at a time.

Plan the Big Picture

Most people start the new school year by filling in birthdays, vacations, and holidays, but don't stop there. You'll also want to make note of the dates for favorite local festivals, science fairs, homeschool days at museums and attractions, and upcoming exhibitions or movies you don't want to miss. We also use our yearly calendar (see close-up below) to keep up with our favorite less-well-known holidays such as Pi Day (March 14), Random Acts of Kindness Day (February 17), and Hobbit Day (September 22). Since we bought our first telescope, we've also included meteor showers, eclipses, and other night sky events on our annual calendar.

YEAR:

Year Calendar ________ YEAR

JULY	AUGUST
14 - Mom's birthday	5 - Ellie's birthday

NOVEMBER	DECEMBER
NANOWRIMO (all month)	
4 - King Tut Day	

MARCH	APRIL

BE AWARE: *Homeschooling is regulated by individual states, not by the federal government—which means different states have different requirements. Some states ask homeschoolers to register and report attendance, some require homeschoolers to register with an umbrella school or have their curriculum approved, and others don't have official requirements. Make sure you understand and comply with your particular state's homeschool laws. (Local homeschool groups are a great resource if you are confused about a specific requirement.) You'll want to make sure all your important dates for homeschool paperwork are noted on your annual calendar.*

Once you've mapped out the year's big events, turn your attention to your goals for the year. Some of your goals are probably academic and student-specific—finally get a handle on handwriting, master the multiplication table, practice the five-paragraph paper. Some of your goals for your students might be more personal—find a social group, reduce math anxiety, learn to manage deadlines and due dates effectively. Other goals may focus on your general homeschool—find a way to work in more art history, set up a dedicated homeschool space, establish a productive routine. If this is your first year homeschooling, your goals may be more minimalist—make it through the year, gain homeschool confidence. It's okay to think as big or small as you want to—these are your goals, and you get to decide what they are.

As the months pass, you may find yourself revisiting these pages and tweaking your goals to better reflect your homeschool—that's great! Having a vision helps you focus on the big picture, but that doesn't mean your big picture has to be static. You shouldn't be surprised if you find yourself wanting to make some adjustments to your plan as your homeschool finds its rhythm. In fact, it would probably be surprising if you didn't improve on your plan for the year at some point.

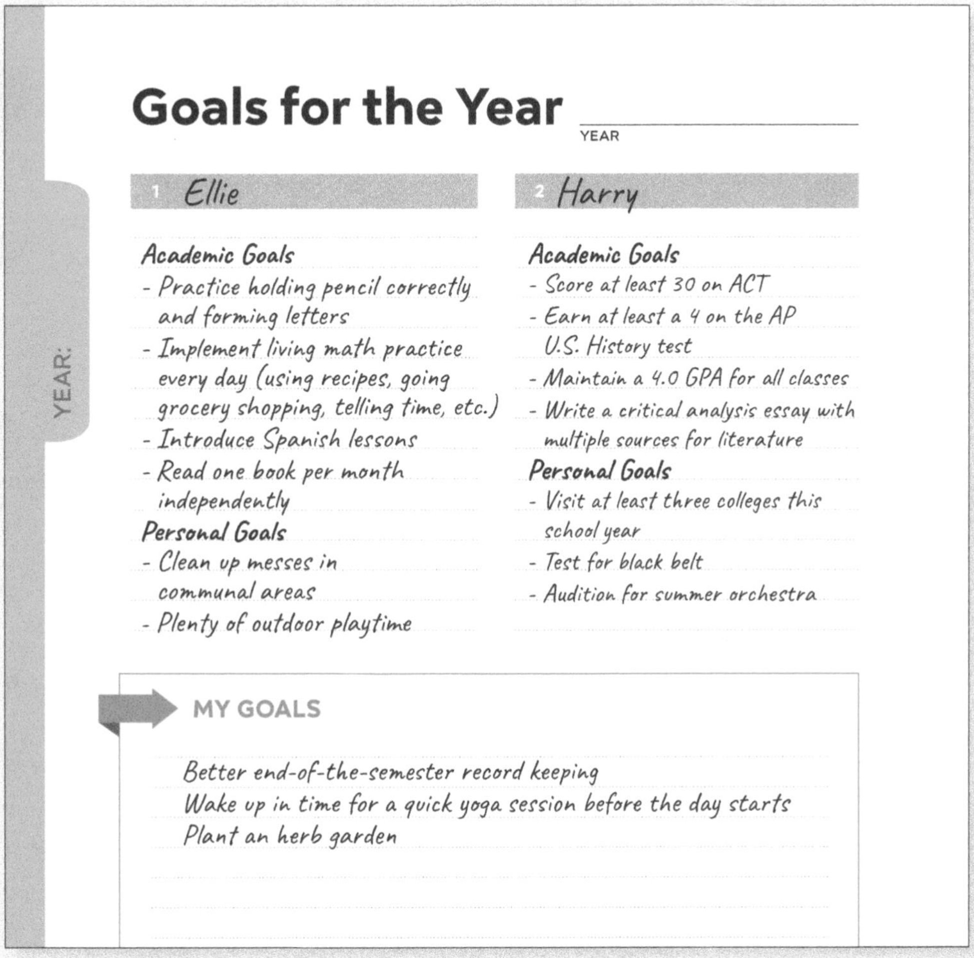

YEAR:

Goals for the Year ____________ YEAR

1 *Ellie*

Academic Goals
- *Practice holding pencil correctly and forming letters*
- *Implement living math practice every day (using recipes, going grocery shopping, telling time, etc.)*
- *Introduce Spanish lessons*
- *Read one book per month independently*

Personal Goals
- *Clean up messes in communal areas*
- *Plenty of outdoor playtime*

2 *Harry*

Academic Goals
- *Score at least 30 on ACT*
- *Earn at least a 4 on the AP U.S. History test*
- *Maintain a 4.0 GPA for all classes*
- *Write a critical analysis essay with multiple sources for literature*

Personal Goals
- *Visit at least three colleges this school year*
- *Test for black belt*
- *Audition for summer orchestra*

MY GOALS

Better end-of-the-semester record keeping
Wake up in time for a quick yoga session before the day starts
Plant an herb garden

Master the Months

Once you've planned your year, you're ready to break things down into monthly increments. Use these pages for a quick visual overview of your month—you can easily see recurring classes and activities, field trips and festivals, and other events you want to keep in mind as you're organizing your month. (I jot down library book due dates and keep track of our current family read-alouds in our monthly calendar, too.)

You'll notice that monthly calendars have their own section instead of being spread out through the weekly sections. There are a few reasons for this. First, not every month has the same number of weeks. Second, it's much easier when you're planning the homeschool co-op's history fair or coordinating a volunteer day for your students to be able to quickly scan all your monthly calendars at once. And finally, if you're tracking monthly attendance—for your own records or to comply with your state's homeschool requirements—this section is an easy, convenient place to do that.

September

MONTH

SUNDAY	MONDAY	TUESDAY	WEDNESDAY
	1 *Ellie - Nature Center Class*	2 *Park Day at Half Moon Park*	3
7	8	9	10 *Library books due*
14	15	16 *Ellie - Girl Scouts*	17 *Homeschool Day at the Art Museum*
21 *Meals on Wheels delivery day*	22	23	24 *Harry - Biology final exam*
28	29	30	31

MONTH: *September*

Work on the Weeks

Now you're ready to tackle the weeks. There are two basic approaches to homeschool planning: You can make a plan at the beginning of each week to follow, or you can move forward at your own pace and use your planner to keep a record of what you've accomplished each day. Whichever way you choose, you'll find plenty of space to track a full schedule of core subjects and extra-curriculars for up to six students. Following each weekly schedule spread, you'll find space to keep up with all your extras: family read-alouds and independent reading, field trips, outside classes, and anything else that's important to your homeschool. You'll also find a place to record grades or notes about your

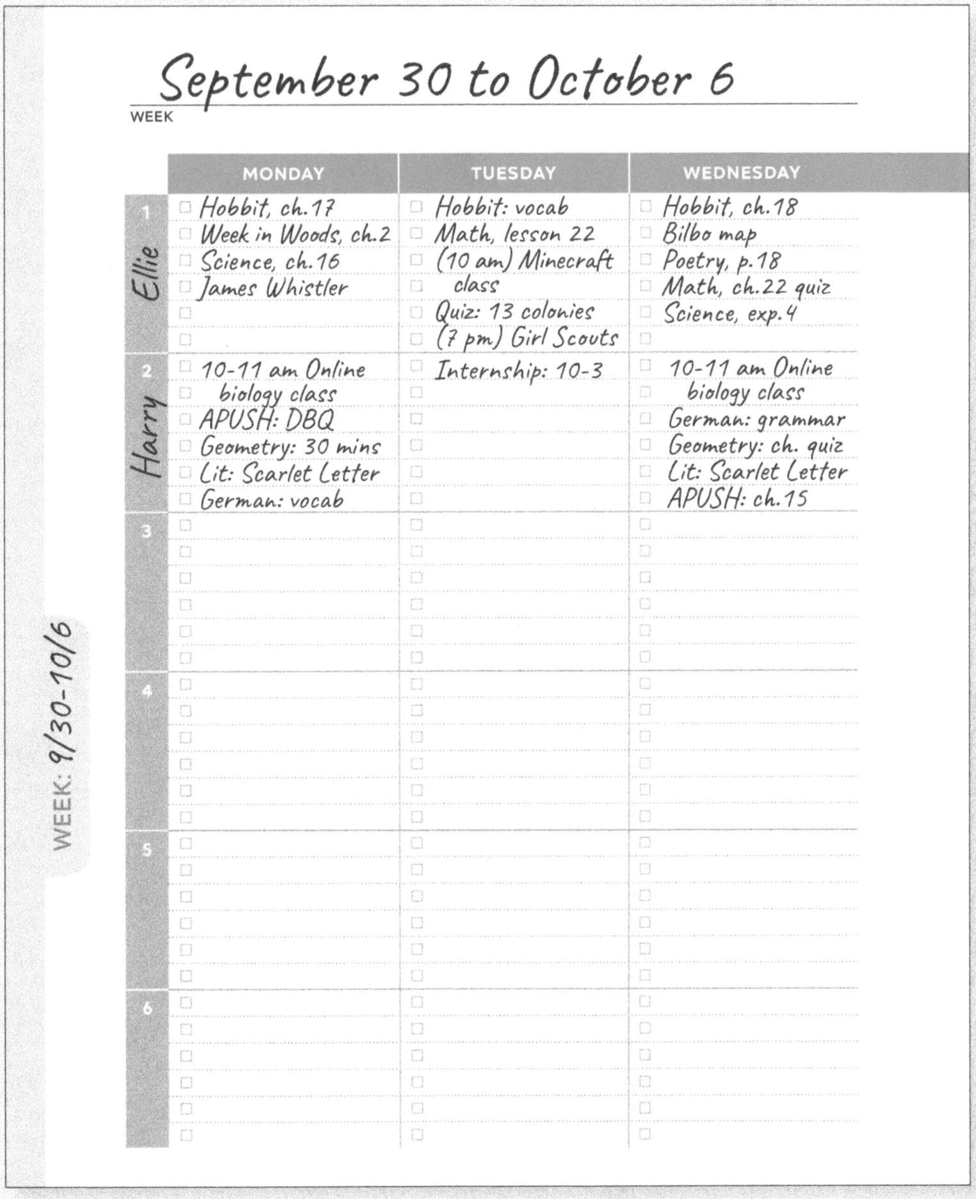
September 30 to October 6
WEEK

	MONDAY	TUESDAY	WEDNESDAY
1 Ellie	Hobbit, ch.17 Week in Woods, ch.2 Science, ch.16 James Whistler	Hobbit: vocab Math, lesson 22 (10 am) Minecraft class Quiz: 13 colonies (7 pm) Girl Scouts	Hobbit, ch.18 Bilbo map Poetry, p.18 Math, ch.22 quiz Science, exp.4
2 Harry	10-11 am Online biology class APUSH: DBQ Geometry: 30 mins Lit: Scarlet Letter German: vocab	Internship: 10-3	10-11 am Online biology class German: grammar Geometry: ch. quiz Lit: Scarlet Letter APUSH: ch.15
3			
4			
5			
6			

WEEK: 9/30-10/6

students' progress. You may keep letter grades for every subject, especially as your student gets older, or use the grade spaces to record big projects and learning milestones. Whatever your preferred method, these pages will give you a snapshot of your students' academic progress over the course of the school year.

These pages are the heart of the planner, so feel free to adapt them as you learn what works best for your students.

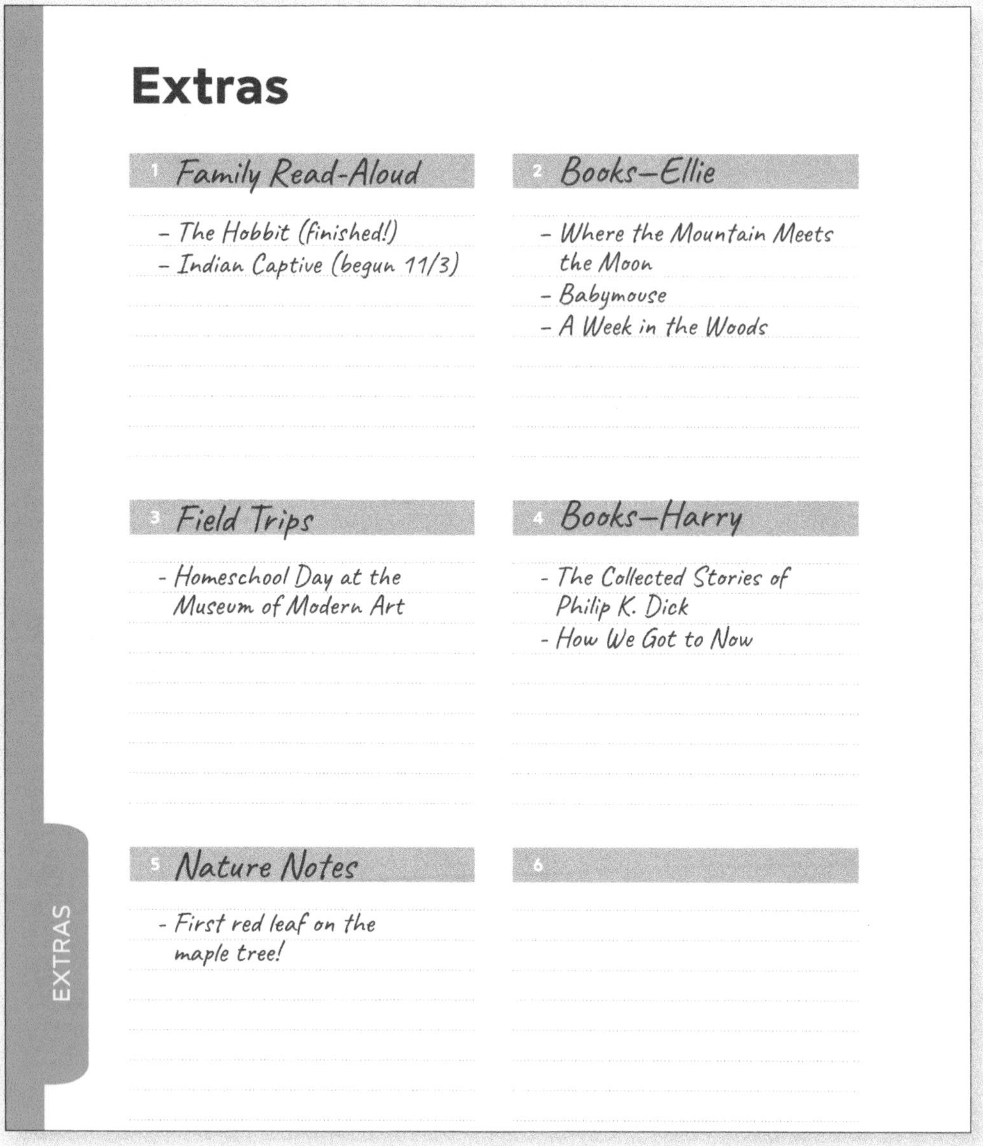

Extras

1 *Family Read-Aloud*

- *The Hobbit (finished!)*
- *Indian Captive (begun 11/3)*

2 *Books—Ellie*

- *Where the Mountain Meets the Moon*
- *Babymouse*
- *A Week in the Woods*

3 *Field Trips*

- *Homeschool Day at the Museum of Modern Art*

4 *Books—Harry*

- *The Collected Stories of Philip K. Dick*
- *How We Got to Now*

5 *Nature Notes*

- *First red leaf on the maple tree!*

6

EXTRAS

Grades

	SUBJECT	GRADE
1 Ellie	English:	
	Math:	
	Science: Lab Report	
	History: 13 Colonies Quiz -	13/13
	Arts: Whistler portrait turned out great!	
2 Harry	English:	A-
	Math:	
	Science: Chemistry quiz (online)	93/100
	History:	88/100
	Arts: Moved up a level in violin lessons	
3		
4		
5		
6		

GRADES

Revisit the Year

Congratulations! You made it through this year. But your planner doesn't stop here: Now it's time to reflect on the homeschool year you've just completed. What were your big accomplishments? What did you learn? Where do you go from here?

To make the most of this section, set aside a little one-on-one time with each of your students to talk about how the year went for them and to brainstorm ideas for going forward. If your third-grader fell in love with his online classes, you may want to look for more online options for the next academic year; if you realized that your tenth-grader is struggling with answering essay questions, you might want to shop for a high school writing curriculum over the break. This section also helps you shift your perspective back to the big-picture goals you set at the beginning of the year—how successful were you at achieving them, or how did they change over the course of the year?

The Year in Review ____________
YEAR

YEAR:

1 *Ellie*

Ellie really bloomed this year! She read multiple books on her own every month and mastered the basics of handwriting. Spanish did not work out—still want to try this, but maybe with a different curriculum or teacher? Getting more comfortable with math and spending lots of playtime outside, but still need to work on clean-up habits.

2 *Harry*

Harry accomplished most of what we hoped for his 10th grade year. His ACT score was 29, just a point shy of his goal, so planning to retake the test in the fall. He decided not to take the APUSH test, but he scored a 4 on the practice test. His grades for the year averaged a 4.0. Need to find a better option for science labs—this class wasn't a great fit.

3

MY YEAR IN REVIEW

Homeschooling is always a work in progress, and this planner is designed with that in mind. Whether you're a brand-new homeschooler or an experienced homeschool parent, you'll find your homeschool growing and adjusting over the course of the year to better meet the needs of your individual students—after all, that's what homeschooling is all about. With this planner, you can be confident that you're covering your bases and staying focused on what matters most to you, even as your daily or monthly plans change with your experience and opportunities.

Right now, these blank pages are full of possibilities—your homeschool can be whatever you want it to be. And at the end of the year, you'll be able to flip back through these pages to see a tangible record of all that you accomplished and learned together. May this be your happiest homeschool year yet!

Year Calendar

YEAR

YEAR:

JULY

AUGUST

NOVEMBER

DECEMBER

MARCH

APRIL

When children are curious, they learn. Like eager birds, they track, hunt, and pursue knowledge as if it's going out of fashion. They learn autonomously without fear of failure, and whatever they discover is etched in their memories for a lifetime. —AMELIA DASHWOOD

YEAR:

SEPTEMBER	OCTOBER

JANUARY	FEBRUARY

MAY	JUNE

Goals for the Year

YEAR

YEAR:

1	2

MY GOALS

★ If housework feels like it's getting out of control, consider putting it on the schedule. Setting aside 30 minutes to officially clean up lunch or fold laundry can be more effective than trying to do it when you "get a few minutes," which might not happen on any given day.

3

4

5

6

YEAR:

MONTH

SUNDAY	MONDAY	TUESDAY	WEDNESDAY

MONTH:

All education is self-education. A teacher is only a guide, to point out the way, and no school, no matter how excellent, can give you education. What you receive is like the outlines in a child's coloring book. You must fill in the colors yourself. —LOUIS L'AMOUR

THURSDAY	FRIDAY	SATURDAY

ATTENDANCE

NOTES

MONTH:

MONTH

SUNDAY	MONDAY	TUESDAY	WEDNESDAY

MONTH:

★ Keep up with all-day snackers by prepping snacks for the whole week over the weekend. Divide them up into single-serving size containers so kids can grab a snack when they get the munchies without interrupting the flow of learning time.

THURSDAY	FRIDAY	SATURDAY

ATTENDANCE

NOTES

MONTH:

MONTH

SUNDAY	MONDAY	TUESDAY	WEDNESDAY

MONTH:

★ Read aloud every day. Even as kids get older and read more independently, a daily read-aloud is a ritual that the whole family can enjoy.

THURSDAY	FRIDAY	SATURDAY

ATTENDANCE

NOTES

MONTH:

MONTH

SUNDAY	MONDAY	TUESDAY	WEDNESDAY

MONTH:

Have faith that your child's brain is an evolving planet that rotates at its own speed. It will naturally be attracted to or repel certain subjects. Be patient. Just as there are ugly ducklings that turn into beautiful swans, there are rebellious kids and slow learners that turn into serious innovators and hardcore intellectuals. —SUZY KASSEM

THURSDAY	FRIDAY	SATURDAY

ATTENDANCE

NOTES

MONTH:

MONTH

SUNDAY	MONDAY	TUESDAY	WEDNESDAY

MONTH:

★ Keep a Bad Day Box stocked with games, puzzles, fun art supplies, craft kits, Lego sets, and other hands-on activities, and pull a new project out on the days you need a break or when your homeschool feels like it's hit a roadblock.

THURSDAY	FRIDAY	SATURDAY

ATTENDANCE

NOTES

MONTH:

MONTH

SUNDAY	MONDAY	TUESDAY	WEDNESDAY

MONTH:

When the atmosphere encourages learning, the learning is inevitable.
—ELIZABETH FOSS

THURSDAY	FRIDAY	SATURDAY

ATTENDANCE

NOTES

MONTH:

MONTH

SUNDAY	MONDAY	TUESDAY	WEDNESDAY

MONTH:

★ Color-coding can be a busy mom's best friend. If you're homeschooling multiple students, assign each one a color and use it for folders and notebooks, sticky notes and bookmarks, pens and pencils. You'll always be able to tell with a glance whose stuff is where.

THURSDAY	FRIDAY	SATURDAY

ATTENDANCE

NOTES

MONTH:

MONTH

SUNDAY	MONDAY	TUESDAY	WEDNESDAY

MONTH:

Go as far as you can see; when you get there, you'll be able to see farther.

—J.P. MORGAN

THURSDAY	FRIDAY	SATURDAY

ATTENDANCE

NOTES

MONTH:

MONTH

SUNDAY	MONDAY	TUESDAY	WEDNESDAY

MONTH:

★ Every few months, take a few minutes to jot down a "Love It-Hate It-Need It" list for your homeschool. Make a note of what's working great, what's not working at all, and what seems to be missing. You don't have to act on everything in your list, but it will help you stay focused when you *are* ready to make a change.

THURSDAY	FRIDAY	SATURDAY

ATTENDANCE

NOTES

MONTH:

MONTH

SUNDAY	MONDAY	TUESDAY	WEDNESDAY

MONTH:

When you take risks you learn that there will be times when you succeed and there will be times when you fail, and both are equally important. —ELLEN DEGENERES

THURSDAY	FRIDAY	SATURDAY

ATTENDANCE

NOTES

MONTH:

MONTH

SUNDAY	MONDAY	TUESDAY	WEDNESDAY

MONTH:

No one has yet realized the wealth of sympathy, kindness, and generosity hidden in the soul of a child. The effort of every true education should be to unlock that treasure. —EMMA GOLDMAN

THURSDAY	FRIDAY	SATURDAY

ATTENDANCE

NOTES

MONTH:

MONTH

SUNDAY	MONDAY	TUESDAY	WEDNESDAY

MONTH:

Education would be much more effective if its purpose was to ensure that by the time they leave school every boy and girl should know how much they do not know, and be imbued with a lifelong desire to know it. —WILLIAM HALEY

THURSDAY	FRIDAY	SATURDAY

ATTENDANCE

NOTES

MONTH:

WEEK

	MONDAY	TUESDAY	WEDNESDAY
1	☐ ☐ ☐ ☐ ☐ ☐	☐ ☐ ☐ ☐ ☐ ☐	☐ ☐ ☐ ☐ ☐ ☐
2	☐ ☐ ☐ ☐ ☐ ☐	☐ ☐ ☐ ☐ ☐ ☐	☐ ☐ ☐ ☐ ☐ ☐
3	☐ ☐ ☐ ☐ ☐ ☐	☐ ☐ ☐ ☐ ☐ ☐	☐ ☐ ☐ ☐ ☐ ☐
4	☐ ☐ ☐ ☐ ☐ ☐	☐ ☐ ☐ ☐ ☐ ☐	☐ ☐ ☐ ☐ ☐ ☐
5	☐ ☐ ☐ ☐ ☐ ☐	☐ ☐ ☐ ☐ ☐ ☐	☐ ☐ ☐ ☐ ☐ ☐
6	☐ ☐ ☐ ☐ ☐ ☐	☐ ☐ ☐ ☐ ☐ ☐	☐ ☐ ☐ ☐ ☐ ☐

WEEK:

★ Don't worry about socialization. Really. Go to homeschool events, play at park days, talk to families at co-op, plan a few play dates, go grocery shopping, do volunteer work, take a class—your child will be socialized just fine.

THURSDAY	FRIDAY	SAT / SUN
☐	☐	☐
☐	☐	☐
☐	☐	☐
☐	☐	☐
☐	☐	☐
☐	☐	☐
☐	☐	☐
☐	☐	☐
☐	☐	☐
☐	☐	☐
☐	☐	☐
☐	☐	☐
☐	☐	☐
☐	☐	☐
☐	☐	☐
☐	☐	☐
☐	☐	☐
☐	☐	☐
☐	☐	☐
☐	☐	☐
☐	☐	☐
☐	☐	☐
☐	☐	☐
☐	☐	☐
☐	☐	☐
☐	☐	☐
☐	☐	☐
☐	☐	☐
☐	☐	☐
☐	☐	☐
☐	☐	☐
☐	☐	☐
☐	☐	☐
☐	☐	☐
☐	☐	☐
☐	☐	☐

WEEK:

Extras

1

2

3

4

5

6

EXTRAS

Grades

★ Attach a pompom to the end of dry erase markers with a dab of hot glue, and you've got an erasable marker for your whiteboard.

	SUBJECT	GRADE
1		
2		
3		
4		
5		
6		

GRADES

WEEK

WEEK:

	MONDAY	TUESDAY	WEDNESDAY
1	☐	☐	☐
	☐	☐	☐
	☐	☐	☐
	☐	☐	☐
	☐	☐	☐
	☐	☐	☐
2	☐	☐	☐
	☐	☐	☐
	☐	☐	☐
	☐	☐	☐
	☐	☐	☐
	☐	☐	☐
3	☐	☐	☐
	☐	☐	☐
	☐	☐	☐
	☐	☐	☐
	☐	☐	☐
	☐	☐	☐
4	☐	☐	☐
	☐	☐	☐
	☐	☐	☐
	☐	☐	☐
	☐	☐	☐
	☐	☐	☐
5	☐	☐	☐
	☐	☐	☐
	☐	☐	☐
	☐	☐	☐
	☐	☐	☐
	☐	☐	☐
6	☐	☐	☐
	☐	☐	☐
	☐	☐	☐
	☐	☐	☐
	☐	☐	☐
	☐	☐	☐

Whatever an education is, it should make you a unique individual, not a conformist; it should furnish you with an original spirit with which to tackle the big challenges. It should allow you to find values which will be your road map through life; it should make you spiritually rich, a person who loves whatever you are doing, wherever you are, whomever you are with; it should teach you what is important, how to live and how to die. —JOHN TAYLOR GATTO

THURSDAY	FRIDAY	SAT / SUN
☐	☐	☐
☐	☐	☐
☐	☐	☐
☐	☐	☐
☐	☐	☐
☐	☐	☐
☐	☐	☐
☐	☐	☐
☐	☐	☐
☐	☐	☐
☐	☐	☐
☐	☐	☐
☐	☐	☐
☐	☐	☐
☐	☐	☐
☐	☐	☐
☐	☐	☐
☐	☐	☐
☐	☐	☐
☐	☐	☐
☐	☐	☐
☐	☐	☐
☐	☐	☐
☐	☐	☐
☐	☐	☐
☐	☐	☐
☐	☐	☐
☐	☐	☐
☐	☐	☐
☐	☐	☐
☐	☐	☐
☐	☐	☐
☐	☐	☐
☐	☐	☐
☐	☐	☐
☐	☐	☐

WEEK:

Extras

1

2

3

4

5

6

EXTRAS

Grades

★ Make everyday activities like doing laundry, budgeting for groceries, or working in the garden part of your homeschool curriculum.

	SUBJECT	GRADE
1		
2		
3		
4		
5		
6		

GRADES

WEEK

	MONDAY	TUESDAY	WEDNESDAY
1	☐	☐	☐
	☐	☐	☐
	☐	☐	☐
	☐	☐	☐
	☐	☐	☐
	☐	☐	☐
2	☐	☐	☐
	☐	☐	☐
	☐	☐	☐
	☐	☐	☐
	☐	☐	☐
	☐	☐	☐
3	☐	☐	☐
	☐	☐	☐
	☐	☐	☐
	☐	☐	☐
	☐	☐	☐
	☐	☐	☐
4	☐	☐	☐
	☐	☐	☐
	☐	☐	☐
	☐	☐	☐
	☐	☐	☐
	☐	☐	☐
5	☐	☐	☐
	☐	☐	☐
	☐	☐	☐
	☐	☐	☐
	☐	☐	☐
	☐	☐	☐
6	☐	☐	☐
	☐	☐	☐
	☐	☐	☐
	☐	☐	☐
	☐	☐	☐
	☐	☐	☐

★ Keep a Joy Journal and write down at least one good thing about each home-school day. Not only will this be a great record of your homeschool life, it's also a powerful mood lifter if you flip back through it when you are having a rough day.

THURSDAY	FRIDAY	SAT / SUN
☐	☐	☐
☐	☐	☐
☐	☐	☐
☐	☐	☐
☐	☐	☐
☐	☐	☐
☐	☐	☐
☐	☐	☐
☐	☐	☐
☐	☐	☐
☐	☐	☐
☐	☐	☐
☐	☐	☐
☐	☐	☐
☐	☐	☐
☐	☐	☐
☐	☐	☐
☐	☐	☐
☐	☐	☐
☐	☐	☐
☐	☐	☐
☐	☐	☐
☐	☐	☐
☐	☐	☐
☐	☐	☐
☐	☐	☐
☐	☐	☐
☐	☐	☐
☐	☐	☐
☐	☐	☐
☐	☐	☐
☐	☐	☐
☐	☐	☐
☐	☐	☐
☐	☐	☐
☐	☐	☐

Extras

1

2

3

4

5

6

EXTRAS

Grades

There is no end to education. It is not that you read a book, pass an examination, and finish with education. The whole of life, from the moment you are born till the moment you die, is a process of learning. —J. KRISHNAMURTI

	SUBJECT	GRADE
1		
2		
3		
4		
5		
6		

GRADES

WEEK

	MONDAY	TUESDAY	WEDNESDAY
1	☐	☐	☐
	☐	☐	☐
	☐	☐	☐
	☐	☐	☐
	☐	☐	☐
	☐	☐	☐
2	☐	☐	☐
	☐	☐	☐
	☐	☐	☐
	☐	☐	☐
	☐	☐	☐
	☐	☐	☐
3	☐	☐	☐
	☐	☐	☐
	☐	☐	☐
	☐	☐	☐
	☐	☐	☐
	☐	☐	☐
4	☐	☐	☐
	☐	☐	☐
	☐	☐	☐
	☐	☐	☐
	☐	☐	☐
	☐	☐	☐
5	☐	☐	☐
	☐	☐	☐
	☐	☐	☐
	☐	☐	☐
	☐	☐	☐
	☐	☐	☐
6	☐	☐	☐
	☐	☐	☐
	☐	☐	☐
	☐	☐	☐
	☐	☐	☐
	☐	☐	☐

★ Resist the urge to move on to the next thing if your child is in love with a particular subject or activity. You don't need to rush.

THURSDAY	FRIDAY	SAT / SUN
☐	☐	☐
☐	☐	☐
☐	☐	☐
☐	☐	☐
☐	☐	☐
☐	☐	☐
☐	☐	☐
☐	☐	☐
☐	☐	☐
☐	☐	☐
☐	☐	☐
☐	☐	☐
☐	☐	☐
☐	☐	☐
☐	☐	☐
☐	☐	☐
☐	☐	☐
☐	☐	☐
☐	☐	☐
☐	☐	☐
☐	☐	☐
☐	☐	☐
☐	☐	☐
☐	☐	☐
☐	☐	☐
☐	☐	☐
☐	☐	☐
☐	☐	☐
☐	☐	☐
☐	☐	☐
☐	☐	☐
☐	☐	☐
☐	☐	☐
☐	☐	☐
☐	☐	☐
☐	☐	☐

WEEK:

Extras

1

2

3

4

5

6

EXTRAS

Grades

What you learn today, for no reason at all, will help you discover all the wonderful secrets of tomorrow.
—NORMAN JUSTER

	SUBJECT	GRADE
1		
2		
3		
4		
5		
6		

GRADES

WEEK

	MONDAY	TUESDAY	WEDNESDAY
1	☐ ☐ ☐ ☐ ☐ ☐	☐ ☐ ☐ ☐ ☐ ☐	☐ ☐ ☐ ☐ ☐ ☐
2	☐ ☐ ☐ ☐ ☐ ☐	☐ ☐ ☐ ☐ ☐ ☐	☐ ☐ ☐ ☐ ☐ ☐
3	☐ ☐ ☐ ☐ ☐ ☐	☐ ☐ ☐ ☐ ☐ ☐	☐ ☐ ☐ ☐ ☐ ☐
4	☐ ☐ ☐ ☐ ☐ ☐	☐ ☐ ☐ ☐ ☐ ☐	☐ ☐ ☐ ☐ ☐ ☐
5	☐ ☐ ☐ ☐ ☐ ☐	☐ ☐ ☐ ☐ ☐ ☐	☐ ☐ ☐ ☐ ☐ ☐
6	☐ ☐ ☐ ☐ ☐ ☐	☐ ☐ ☐ ☐ ☐ ☐	☐ ☐ ☐ ☐ ☐ ☐

★ Pay attention to what your child enjoys. There's a good chance that the work and activities that get them excited indicate their natural learning style. Once you understand their learning style, you can use it to revolutionize activities or lessons that don't seem to come naturally for them.

THURSDAY	FRIDAY	SAT / SUN
☐	☐	☐
☐	☐	☐
☐	☐	☐
☐	☐	☐
☐	☐	☐
☐	☐	☐
☐	☐	☐
☐	☐	☐
☐	☐	☐
☐	☐	☐
☐	☐	☐
☐	☐	☐
☐	☐	☐
☐	☐	☐
☐	☐	☐
☐	☐	☐
☐	☐	☐
☐	☐	☐
☐	☐	☐
☐	☐	☐
☐	☐	☐
☐	☐	☐
☐	☐	☐
☐	☐	☐
☐	☐	☐
☐	☐	☐
☐	☐	☐
☐	☐	☐
☐	☐	☐
☐	☐	☐
☐	☐	☐
☐	☐	☐
☐	☐	☐
☐	☐	☐
☐	☐	☐
☐	☐	☐

WEEK:

Extras

1

2

3

4

5

6

EXTRAS

Grades

★ Don't spend a lot of money on curriculum items for the future. It's very likely that you will change your mind at least half a dozen times about what you want to do between now and then.

	SUBJECT	GRADE
1		
2		
3		
4		
5		
6		

WEEK

	MONDAY	TUESDAY	WEDNESDAY
1			
2			
3			
4			
5			
6			

WEEK:

We can think of ourselves not as teachers but as gardeners. A gardener does not grow flowers; he tries to give them what he thinks they need, and they grow by themselves. —JOHN HOLT

THURSDAY	FRIDAY	SAT / SUN
☐	☐	☐
☐	☐	☐
☐	☐	☐
☐	☐	☐
☐	☐	☐
☐	☐	☐
☐	☐	☐
☐	☐	☐
☐	☐	☐
☐	☐	☐
☐	☐	☐
☐	☐	☐
☐	☐	☐
☐	☐	☐
☐	☐	☐
☐	☐	☐
☐	☐	☐
☐	☐	☐
☐	☐	☐
☐	☐	☐
☐	☐	☐
☐	☐	☐
☐	☐	☐
☐	☐	☐
☐	☐	☐
☐	☐	☐
☐	☐	☐
☐	☐	☐
☐	☐	☐
☐	☐	☐
☐	☐	☐
☐	☐	☐
☐	☐	☐
☐	☐	☐
☐	☐	☐
☐	☐	☐

WEEK:

Extras

1

2

3

4

5

6

EXTRAS

Grades

In teaching you cannot see the fruit of a day's work.
It is invisible and remains so, maybe for twenty years.
—JACQUES BARZUN

	SUBJECT	GRADE
1		
2		
3		
4		
5		
6		

WEEK

	MONDAY	TUESDAY	WEDNESDAY
1	☐	☐	☐
	☐	☐	☐
	☐	☐	☐
	☐	☐	☐
	☐	☐	☐
	☐	☐	☐
2	☐	☐	☐
	☐	☐	☐
	☐	☐	☐
	☐	☐	☐
	☐	☐	☐
	☐	☐	☐
3	☐	☐	☐
	☐	☐	☐
	☐	☐	☐
	☐	☐	☐
	☐	☐	☐
	☐	☐	☐
4	☐	☐	☐
	☐	☐	☐
	☐	☐	☐
	☐	☐	☐
	☐	☐	☐
	☐	☐	☐
5	☐	☐	☐
	☐	☐	☐
	☐	☐	☐
	☐	☐	☐
	☐	☐	☐
	☐	☐	☐
6	☐	☐	☐
	☐	☐	☐
	☐	☐	☐
	☐	☐	☐
	☐	☐	☐
	☐	☐	☐

WEEK:

★ Let go of the idea of "grade level." It's okay if your second-grader isn't ready to read or if your kindergartner is reading fourth-grade books. Don't pin yourself down with a preconceived list of things your child needs to learn at a certain time.

THURSDAY	FRIDAY	SAT / SUN
☐	☐	☐
☐	☐	☐
☐	☐	☐
☐	☐	☐
☐	☐	☐
☐	☐	☐
☐	☐	☐
☐	☐	☐
☐	☐	☐
☐	☐	☐
☐	☐	☐
☐	☐	☐
☐	☐	☐
☐	☐	☐
☐	☐	☐
☐	☐	☐
☐	☐	☐
☐	☐	☐
☐	☐	☐
☐	☐	☐
☐	☐	☐
☐	☐	☐
☐	☐	☐
☐	☐	☐
☐	☐	☐
☐	☐	☐
☐	☐	☐
☐	☐	☐
☐	☐	☐
☐	☐	☐
☐	☐	☐
☐	☐	☐
☐	☐	☐
☐	☐	☐
☐	☐	☐
☐	☐	☐

WEEK:

Extras

1

2

3

4

5

6

EXTRAS

Grades

★ Homeschooling is like "learning concentrate," and you can get a lot done in an hour. Don't be surprised if your homeschool lessons take less time than you initially schedule.

	SUBJECT	GRADE
1		
2		
3		
4		
5		
6		

WEEK

	MONDAY	TUESDAY	WEDNESDAY
1	☐	☐	☐
	☐	☐	☐
	☐	☐	☐
	☐	☐	☐
	☐	☐	☐
	☐	☐	☐
2	☐	☐	☐
	☐	☐	☐
	☐	☐	☐
	☐	☐	☐
	☐	☐	☐
	☐	☐	☐
3	☐	☐	☐
	☐	☐	☐
	☐	☐	☐
	☐	☐	☐
	☐	☐	☐
	☐	☐	☐
4	☐	☐	☐
	☐	☐	☐
	☐	☐	☐
	☐	☐	☐
	☐	☐	☐
	☐	☐	☐
5	☐	☐	☐
	☐	☐	☐
	☐	☐	☐
	☐	☐	☐
	☐	☐	☐
	☐	☐	☐
6	☐	☐	☐
	☐	☐	☐
	☐	☐	☐
	☐	☐	☐
	☐	☐	☐
	☐	☐	☐

★ Resist the urge to compare your homeschool to anyone else's. Inevitably, you'll be comparing your worst days to someone else's best days, and you'll just end up feeling insecure and frustrated. Instead, shift your focus to *your* big picture and how successfully you're reaching the goals you've set for yourself.

THURSDAY	FRIDAY	SAT / SUN
☐	☐	☐
☐	☐	☐
☐	☐	☐
☐	☐	☐
☐	☐	☐
☐	☐	☐
☐	☐	☐
☐	☐	☐
☐	☐	☐
☐	☐	☐
☐	☐	☐
☐	☐	☐
☐	☐	☐
☐	☐	☐
☐	☐	☐
☐	☐	☐
☐	☐	☐
☐	☐	☐
☐	☐	☐
☐	☐	☐
☐	☐	☐
☐	☐	☐
☐	☐	☐
☐	☐	☐
☐	☐	☐
☐	☐	☐
☐	☐	☐
☐	☐	☐
☐	☐	☐
☐	☐	☐
☐	☐	☐
☐	☐	☐
☐	☐	☐
☐	☐	☐
☐	☐	☐
☐	☐	☐

WEEK:

Extras

1

2

3

4

5

6

EXTRAS

Grades

I had discovered that learning something, no matter how complex, wasn't hard when I had a reason to want to know it.
—HOMER HICKAM

	SUBJECT	GRADE
1		
2		
3		
4		
5		
6		

WEEK

	MONDAY	TUESDAY	WEDNESDAY
1	☐	☐	☐
	☐	☐	☐
	☐	☐	☐
	☐	☐	☐
	☐	☐	☐
	☐	☐	☐
2	☐	☐	☐
	☐	☐	☐
	☐	☐	☐
	☐	☐	☐
	☐	☐	☐
	☐	☐	☐
3	☐	☐	☐
	☐	☐	☐
	☐	☐	☐
	☐	☐	☐
	☐	☐	☐
	☐	☐	☐
4	☐	☐	☐
	☐	☐	☐
	☐	☐	☐
	☐	☐	☐
	☐	☐	☐
	☐	☐	☐
5	☐	☐	☐
	☐	☐	☐
	☐	☐	☐
	☐	☐	☐
	☐	☐	☐
	☐	☐	☐
6	☐	☐	☐
	☐	☐	☐
	☐	☐	☐
	☐	☐	☐
	☐	☐	☐
	☐	☐	☐

★ Take some personality tests—such as the Myers-Briggs test or an emotional intelligence test—with your child and compare results. Use the opportunity to get to know each other and the best ways to work together.

THURSDAY	FRIDAY	SAT / SUN
☐	☐	☐
☐	☐	☐
☐	☐	☐
☐	☐	☐
☐	☐	☐
☐	☐	☐
☐	☐	☐
☐	☐	☐
☐	☐	☐
☐	☐	☐
☐	☐	☐
☐	☐	☐
☐	☐	☐
☐	☐	☐
☐	☐	☐
☐	☐	☐
☐	☐	☐
☐	☐	☐
☐	☐	☐
☐	☐	☐
☐	☐	☐
☐	☐	☐
☐	☐	☐
☐	☐	☐
☐	☐	☐
☐	☐	☐
☐	☐	☐
☐	☐	☐
☐	☐	☐
☐	☐	☐
☐	☐	☐
☐	☐	☐
☐	☐	☐
☐	☐	☐
☐	☐	☐
☐	☐	☐

WEEK:

Extras

1

2

3

4

5

6

EXTRAS

Grades

★ Provide plenty of physical outlets for your child's energy. Organized teams, private lessons, or even a new bike can help set kids on a healthy path toward adulthood.

	SUBJECT	GRADE
1		
2		
3		
4		
5		
6		

GRADES

WEEK

	MONDAY	TUESDAY	WEDNESDAY
1	☐	☐	☐
	☐	☐	☐
	☐	☐	☐
	☐	☐	☐
	☐	☐	☐
	☐	☐	☐
2	☐	☐	☐
	☐	☐	☐
	☐	☐	☐
	☐	☐	☐
	☐	☐	☐
	☐	☐	☐
3	☐	☐	☐
	☐	☐	☐
	☐	☐	☐
	☐	☐	☐
	☐	☐	☐
	☐	☐	☐
4	☐	☐	☐
	☐	☐	☐
	☐	☐	☐
	☐	☐	☐
	☐	☐	☐
	☐	☐	☐
5	☐	☐	☐
	☐	☐	☐
	☐	☐	☐
	☐	☐	☐
	☐	☐	☐
	☐	☐	☐
6	☐	☐	☐
	☐	☐	☐
	☐	☐	☐
	☐	☐	☐
	☐	☐	☐
	☐	☐	☐

★ Schedule downtime for yourself. Homeschooling can start to feel like extreme parenting when you're on duty all day, every day. You will burn out if you don't give yourself a break.

THURSDAY	FRIDAY	SAT / SUN
☐	☐	☐
☐	☐	☐
☐	☐	☐
☐	☐	☐
☐	☐	☐
☐	☐	☐
☐	☐	☐
☐	☐	☐
☐	☐	☐
☐	☐	☐
☐	☐	☐
☐	☐	☐
☐	☐	☐
☐	☐	☐
☐	☐	☐
☐	☐	☐
☐	☐	☐
☐	☐	☐
☐	☐	☐
☐	☐	☐
☐	☐	☐
☐	☐	☐
☐	☐	☐
☐	☐	☐
☐	☐	☐
☐	☐	☐
☐	☐	☐
☐	☐	☐
☐	☐	☐
☐	☐	☐
☐	☐	☐
☐	☐	☐
☐	☐	☐
☐	☐	☐
☐	☐	☐
☐	☐	☐

WEEK:

Extras

1

2

3

4

5

6

EXTRAS

Grades

One learns from books and example only that certain things can be done. Actual learning requires that you do those things. —FRANK HERBERT

	SUBJECT	GRADE
1		
2		
3		
4		
5		
6		

WEEK

	MONDAY	TUESDAY	WEDNESDAY
1	☐ ☐ ☐ ☐ ☐ ☐	☐ ☐ ☐ ☐ ☐ ☐	☐ ☐ ☐ ☐ ☐ ☐
2	☐ ☐ ☐ ☐ ☐ ☐	☐ ☐ ☐ ☐ ☐ ☐	☐ ☐ ☐ ☐ ☐ ☐
3	☐ ☐ ☐ ☐ ☐ ☐	☐ ☐ ☐ ☐ ☐ ☐	☐ ☐ ☐ ☐ ☐ ☐
4	☐ ☐ ☐ ☐ ☐ ☐	☐ ☐ ☐ ☐ ☐ ☐	☐ ☐ ☐ ☐ ☐ ☐
5	☐ ☐ ☐ ☐ ☐ ☐	☐ ☐ ☐ ☐ ☐ ☐	☐ ☐ ☐ ☐ ☐ ☐
6	☐ ☐ ☐ ☐ ☐ ☐	☐ ☐ ☐ ☐ ☐ ☐	☐ ☐ ☐ ☐ ☐ ☐

★ Do what you and your children love doing, and the learning will follow. You'll find opportunities to practice reading, writing, math, and other subjects in everything you do, so do what brings you joy and let learning flow naturally.

THURSDAY	FRIDAY	SAT / SUN
☐	☐	☐
☐	☐	☐
☐	☐	☐
☐	☐	☐
☐	☐	☐
☐	☐	☐
☐	☐	☐
☐	☐	☐
☐	☐	☐
☐	☐	☐
☐	☐	☐
☐	☐	☐
☐	☐	☐
☐	☐	☐
☐	☐	☐
☐	☐	☐
☐	☐	☐
☐	☐	☐
☐	☐	☐
☐	☐	☐
☐	☐	☐
☐	☐	☐
☐	☐	☐
☐	☐	☐
☐	☐	☐
☐	☐	☐
☐	☐	☐
☐	☐	☐
☐	☐	☐
☐	☐	☐
☐	☐	☐
☐	☐	☐
☐	☐	☐
☐	☐	☐
☐	☐	☐
☐	☐	☐

WEEK:

Extras

1

2

3

4

5

6

EXTRAS

Grades

The true test of intelligence is not how much we know how to do, but how to behave when we don't know what to do.
—JOHN HOLT

	SUBJECT	GRADE
1		
2		
3		
4		
5		
6		

WEEK

	MONDAY	TUESDAY	WEDNESDAY
1	☐ ☐ ☐ ☐ ☐ ☐	☐ ☐ ☐ ☐ ☐ ☐	☐ ☐ ☐ ☐ ☐ ☐
2	☐ ☐ ☐ ☐ ☐ ☐	☐ ☐ ☐ ☐ ☐ ☐	☐ ☐ ☐ ☐ ☐ ☐
3	☐ ☐ ☐ ☐ ☐ ☐	☐ ☐ ☐ ☐ ☐ ☐	☐ ☐ ☐ ☐ ☐ ☐
4	☐ ☐ ☐ ☐ ☐ ☐	☐ ☐ ☐ ☐ ☐ ☐	☐ ☐ ☐ ☐ ☐ ☐
5	☐ ☐ ☐ ☐ ☐ ☐	☐ ☐ ☐ ☐ ☐ ☐	☐ ☐ ☐ ☐ ☐ ☐
6	☐ ☐ ☐ ☐ ☐ ☐	☐ ☐ ☐ ☐ ☐ ☐	☐ ☐ ☐ ☐ ☐ ☐

WEEK:

★ A schedule is great, but if you start to feel like your schedule is running you instead of the other way around, pause, take a deep breath, and go back to the drawing board. It's okay to fall behind or get ahead and adjust your schedule accordingly.

THURSDAY	FRIDAY	SAT / SUN
☐	☐	☐
☐	☐	☐
☐	☐	☐
☐	☐	☐
☐	☐	☐
☐	☐	☐
☐	☐	☐
☐	☐	☐
☐	☐	☐
☐	☐	☐
☐	☐	☐
☐	☐	☐
☐	☐	☐
☐	☐	☐
☐	☐	☐
☐	☐	☐
☐	☐	☐
☐	☐	☐
☐	☐	☐
☐	☐	☐
☐	☐	☐
☐	☐	☐
☐	☐	☐
☐	☐	☐
☐	☐	☐
☐	☐	☐
☐	☐	☐
☐	☐	☐
☐	☐	☐
☐	☐	☐
☐	☐	☐
☐	☐	☐
☐	☐	☐
☐	☐	☐
☐	☐	☐
☐	☐	☐

WEEK:

Extras

1

2

3

4

5

6

EXTRAS

Grades

★ There's no timer on happy homeschooling, so if one day math runs into history time or you miss a day of structured learning for a rare nature hike, relax and go with it. You have all the time you need.

	SUBJECT	GRADE
1		
2		
3		
4		
5		
6		

GRADES

WEEK

	MONDAY	TUESDAY	WEDNESDAY
1	☐ ☐ ☐ ☐ ☐ ☐	☐ ☐ ☐ ☐ ☐ ☐	☐ ☐ ☐ ☐ ☐ ☐
2	☐ ☐ ☐ ☐ ☐ ☐	☐ ☐ ☐ ☐ ☐ ☐	☐ ☐ ☐ ☐ ☐ ☐
3	☐ ☐ ☐ ☐ ☐ ☐	☐ ☐ ☐ ☐ ☐ ☐	☐ ☐ ☐ ☐ ☐ ☐
4	☐ ☐ ☐ ☐ ☐ ☐	☐ ☐ ☐ ☐ ☐ ☐	☐ ☐ ☐ ☐ ☐ ☐
5	☐ ☐ ☐ ☐ ☐ ☐	☐ ☐ ☐ ☐ ☐ ☐	☐ ☐ ☐ ☐ ☐ ☐
6	☐ ☐ ☐ ☐ ☐ ☐	☐ ☐ ☐ ☐ ☐ ☐	☐ ☐ ☐ ☐ ☐ ☐

★ You don't have to teach everything to be a great homeschool parent. If your child advances beyond your own knowledge or if you're always butting heads over a particular subject, look for an outside class or tutor to take over teaching duty so that you can focus on what you're good at teaching.

THURSDAY	FRIDAY	SAT / SUN
☐	☐	☐
☐	☐	☐
☐	☐	☐
☐	☐	☐
☐	☐	☐
☐	☐	☐
☐	☐	☐
☐	☐	☐
☐	☐	☐
☐	☐	☐
☐	☐	☐
☐	☐	☐
☐	☐	☐
☐	☐	☐
☐	☐	☐
☐	☐	☐
☐	☐	☐
☐	☐	☐
☐	☐	☐
☐	☐	☐
☐	☐	☐
☐	☐	☐
☐	☐	☐
☐	☐	☐
☐	☐	☐
☐	☐	☐
☐	☐	☐
☐	☐	☐
☐	☐	☐
☐	☐	☐
☐	☐	☐
☐	☐	☐
☐	☐	☐
☐	☐	☐
☐	☐	☐
☐	☐	☐

WEEK:

Extras

1

2

3

4

5

6

EXTRAS

Grades

The greatest gift you can give another is the purity of your attention. —RICHARD MOSS

	SUBJECT	GRADE
1		
2		
3		
4		
5		
6		

GRADES

WEEK

	MONDAY	TUESDAY	WEDNESDAY
1	☐	☐	☐
	☐	☐	☐
	☐	☐	☐
	☐	☐	☐
	☐	☐	☐
	☐	☐	☐
2	☐	☐	☐
	☐	☐	☐
	☐	☐	☐
	☐	☐	☐
	☐	☐	☐
	☐	☐	☐
3	☐	☐	☐
	☐	☐	☐
	☐	☐	☐
	☐	☐	☐
	☐	☐	☐
	☐	☐	☐
4	☐	☐	☐
	☐	☐	☐
	☐	☐	☐
	☐	☐	☐
	☐	☐	☐
	☐	☐	☐
5	☐	☐	☐
	☐	☐	☐
	☐	☐	☐
	☐	☐	☐
	☐	☐	☐
	☐	☐	☐
6	☐	☐	☐
	☐	☐	☐
	☐	☐	☐
	☐	☐	☐
	☐	☐	☐
	☐	☐	☐

WEEK:

★ Find a few daily rituals to anchor your day. Rituals create rhythm and points of connection for you and your students. Good ritual options include nature walks, read-alouds, afternoon tea, and art time.

THURSDAY	FRIDAY	SAT / SUN
☐	☐	☐
☐	☐	☐
☐	☐	☐
☐	☐	☐
☐	☐	☐
☐	☐	☐
☐	☐	☐
☐	☐	☐
☐	☐	☐
☐	☐	☐
☐	☐	☐
☐	☐	☐
☐	☐	☐
☐	☐	☐
☐	☐	☐
☐	☐	☐
☐	☐	☐
☐	☐	☐
☐	☐	☐
☐	☐	☐
☐	☐	☐
☐	☐	☐
☐	☐	☐
☐	☐	☐
☐	☐	☐
☐	☐	☐
☐	☐	☐
☐	☐	☐
☐	☐	☐
☐	☐	☐
☐	☐	☐
☐	☐	☐
☐	☐	☐
☐	☐	☐
☐	☐	☐
☐	☐	☐

WEEK:

Extras

1

2

3

4

5

6

EXTRAS

Grades

★ When a subject hits a major roadblock, consider taking a couple of weeks off to focus on other things. Often, a little break is all you need to spark a breakthrough when you pick back up.

	SUBJECT	GRADE
1		
2		
3		
4		
5		
6		

GRADES

WEEK

	MONDAY	TUESDAY	WEDNESDAY
1	☐	☐	☐
	☐	☐	☐
	☐	☐	☐
	☐	☐	☐
	☐	☐	☐
	☐	☐	☐
2	☐	☐	☐
	☐	☐	☐
	☐	☐	☐
	☐	☐	☐
	☐	☐	☐
	☐	☐	☐
3	☐	☐	☐
	☐	☐	☐
	☐	☐	☐
	☐	☐	☐
	☐	☐	☐
	☐	☐	☐
4	☐	☐	☐
	☐	☐	☐
	☐	☐	☐
	☐	☐	☐
	☐	☐	☐
	☐	☐	☐
5	☐	☐	☐
	☐	☐	☐
	☐	☐	☐
	☐	☐	☐
	☐	☐	☐
	☐	☐	☐
6	☐	☐	☐
	☐	☐	☐
	☐	☐	☐
	☐	☐	☐
	☐	☐	☐
	☐	☐	☐

How different our lives are when we really know what is deeply important to us, and keeping that picture in mind, we manage ourselves each day to be and to do what really matters most. —STEPHEN COVEY

THURSDAY	FRIDAY	SAT / SUN
☐	☐	☐
☐	☐	☐
☐	☐	☐
☐	☐	☐
☐	☐	☐
☐	☐	☐
☐	☐	☐
☐	☐	☐
☐	☐	☐
☐	☐	☐
☐	☐	☐
☐	☐	☐
☐	☐	☐
☐	☐	☐
☐	☐	☐
☐	☐	☐
☐	☐	☐
☐	☐	☐
☐	☐	☐
☐	☐	☐
☐	☐	☐
☐	☐	☐
☐	☐	☐
☐	☐	☐
☐	☐	☐
☐	☐	☐
☐	☐	☐
☐	☐	☐
☐	☐	☐
☐	☐	☐
☐	☐	☐
☐	☐	☐
☐	☐	☐
☐	☐	☐
☐	☐	☐
☐	☐	☐

WEEK:

Extras

1

2

3

4

5

6

EXTRAS

Grades

It may be that when we no longer know what to do, we have come to our real work and when we no longer know which way to go, we have begun our real journey. —WENDELL BERRY

	SUBJECT	GRADE
1		
2		
3		
4		
5		
6		

GRADES

WEEK

	MONDAY	TUESDAY	WEDNESDAY
1	☐	☐	☐
	☐	☐	☐
	☐	☐	☐
	☐	☐	☐
	☐	☐	☐
	☐	☐	☐
2	☐	☐	☐
	☐	☐	☐
	☐	☐	☐
	☐	☐	☐
	☐	☐	☐
	☐	☐	☐
3	☐	☐	☐
	☐	☐	☐
	☐	☐	☐
	☐	☐	☐
	☐	☐	☐
	☐	☐	☐
4	☐	☐	☐
	☐	☐	☐
	☐	☐	☐
	☐	☐	☐
	☐	☐	☐
	☐	☐	☐
5	☐	☐	☐
	☐	☐	☐
	☐	☐	☐
	☐	☐	☐
	☐	☐	☐
	☐	☐	☐
6	☐	☐	☐
	☐	☐	☐
	☐	☐	☐
	☐	☐	☐
	☐	☐	☐
	☐	☐	☐

★ When you're budgeting, spend the most on what your children love, whether that's drama classes or science labs. You can always find free or inexpensive resources for core subjects, so focus your spending where it can have the biggest happiness impact.

THURSDAY	FRIDAY	SAT / SUN
☐	☐	☐
☐	☐	☐
☐	☐	☐
☐	☐	☐
☐	☐	☐
☐	☐	☐
☐	☐	☐
☐	☐	☐
☐	☐	☐
☐	☐	☐
☐	☐	☐
☐	☐	☐
☐	☐	☐
☐	☐	☐
☐	☐	☐
☐	☐	☐
☐	☐	☐
☐	☐	☐
☐	☐	☐
☐	☐	☐
☐	☐	☐
☐	☐	☐
☐	☐	☐
☐	☐	☐
☐	☐	☐
☐	☐	☐
☐	☐	☐
☐	☐	☐
☐	☐	☐
☐	☐	☐
☐	☐	☐
☐	☐	☐
☐	☐	☐
☐	☐	☐
☐	☐	☐
☐	☐	☐

WEEK:

Extras

1

2

3

4

5

6

EXTRAS

Grades

How can you know what you are capable of if you don't embrace the unknown? —ESMERELDA SANTIAGO

	SUBJECT	GRADE
1		
2		
3		
4		
5		
6		

WEEK

	MONDAY	TUESDAY	WEDNESDAY
1			
2			
3			
4			
5			
6			

WEEK:

★ Studies show that homeschoolers excel in college, but preparing your home-schooler for college can feel stressful. One strategy: Jot down the requirements for the most competitive school that's piqued your student's interest, and use those as a guide for planning high school.

THURSDAY	FRIDAY	SAT / SUN
☐	☐	☐
☐	☐	☐
☐	☐	☐
☐	☐	☐
☐	☐	☐
☐	☐	☐
☐	☐	☐
☐	☐	☐
☐	☐	☐
☐	☐	☐
☐	☐	☐
☐	☐	☐
☐	☐	☐
☐	☐	☐
☐	☐	☐
☐	☐	☐
☐	☐	☐
☐	☐	☐
☐	☐	☐
☐	☐	☐
☐	☐	☐
☐	☐	☐
☐	☐	☐
☐	☐	☐
☐	☐	☐
☐	☐	☐
☐	☐	☐
☐	☐	☐
☐	☐	☐
☐	☐	☐
☐	☐	☐
☐	☐	☐
☐	☐	☐
☐	☐	☐
☐	☐	☐
☐	☐	☐

WEEK:

Extras

1

2

3

4

5

6

EXTRAS

Grades

We learn more by looking for the answer to a question and not finding it than we do from learning the answer itself.
—LLOYD ALEXANDER

	SUBJECT	GRADE
1		
2		
3		
4		
5		
6		

GRADES

WEEK

	MONDAY	TUESDAY	WEDNESDAY
1	☐	☐	☐
	☐	☐	☐
	☐	☐	☐
	☐	☐	☐
	☐	☐	☐
	☐	☐	☐
2	☐	☐	☐
	☐	☐	☐
	☐	☐	☐
	☐	☐	☐
	☐	☐	☐
	☐	☐	☐
3	☐	☐	☐
	☐	☐	☐
	☐	☐	☐
	☐	☐	☐
	☐	☐	☐
	☐	☐	☐
4	☐	☐	☐
	☐	☐	☐
	☐	☐	☐
	☐	☐	☐
	☐	☐	☐
	☐	☐	☐
5	☐	☐	☐
	☐	☐	☐
	☐	☐	☐
	☐	☐	☐
	☐	☐	☐
	☐	☐	☐
6	☐	☐	☐
	☐	☐	☐
	☐	☐	☐
	☐	☐	☐
	☐	☐	☐
	☐	☐	☐

★ Let your students fail sometimes. It's tempting to remind them of every forgotten deadline or push them to study when they're not inclined to do so, but now's the time when they can fail and learn from that failure with minimal consequences.

THURSDAY	FRIDAY	SAT / SUN
☐	☐	☐
☐	☐	☐
☐	☐	☐
☐	☐	☐
☐	☐	☐
☐	☐	☐
☐	☐	☐
☐	☐	☐
☐	☐	☐
☐	☐	☐
☐	☐	☐
☐	☐	☐
☐	☐	☐
☐	☐	☐
☐	☐	☐
☐	☐	☐
☐	☐	☐
☐	☐	☐
☐	☐	☐
☐	☐	☐
☐	☐	☐
☐	☐	☐
☐	☐	☐
☐	☐	☐
☐	☐	☐
☐	☐	☐
☐	☐	☐
☐	☐	☐
☐	☐	☐
☐	☐	☐
☐	☐	☐
☐	☐	☐
☐	☐	☐
☐	☐	☐
☐	☐	☐
☐	☐	☐

WEEK:

Extras

1

2

3

4

5

6

EXTRAS

Grades

Your assumptions are your windows on the world. Scrub them off every once in a while, or the light won't come in.
—ISAAC ASIMOV

	SUBJECT	GRADE
1		
2		
3		
4		
5		
6		

WEEK

	MONDAY	TUESDAY	WEDNESDAY
1	☐	☐	☐
	☐	☐	☐
	☐	☐	☐
	☐	☐	☐
	☐	☐	☐
	☐	☐	☐
2	☐	☐	☐
	☐	☐	☐
	☐	☐	☐
	☐	☐	☐
	☐	☐	☐
	☐	☐	☐
3	☐	☐	☐
	☐	☐	☐
	☐	☐	☐
	☐	☐	☐
	☐	☐	☐
	☐	☐	☐
4	☐	☐	☐
	☐	☐	☐
	☐	☐	☐
	☐	☐	☐
	☐	☐	☐
	☐	☐	☐
5	☐	☐	☐
	☐	☐	☐
	☐	☐	☐
	☐	☐	☐
	☐	☐	☐
	☐	☐	☐
6	☐	☐	☐
	☐	☐	☐
	☐	☐	☐
	☐	☐	☐
	☐	☐	☐
	☐	☐	☐

★ If you're having trouble finding a routine for your days, try this: Start with one thing. Make a point of doing it every single day, and once it's a comfortable habit, add something else. Keep adding things, one at a time, until your schedule reflects your goals for the year.

THURSDAY	FRIDAY	SAT / SUN
☐	☐	☐
☐	☐	☐
☐	☐	☐
☐	☐	☐
☐	☐	☐
☐	☐	☐
☐	☐	☐
☐	☐	☐
☐	☐	☐
☐	☐	☐
☐	☐	☐
☐	☐	☐
☐	☐	☐
☐	☐	☐
☐	☐	☐
☐	☐	☐
☐	☐	☐
☐	☐	☐
☐	☐	☐
☐	☐	☐
☐	☐	☐
☐	☐	☐
☐	☐	☐
☐	☐	☐
☐	☐	☐
☐	☐	☐
☐	☐	☐
☐	☐	☐
☐	☐	☐
☐	☐	☐
☐	☐	☐
☐	☐	☐
☐	☐	☐
☐	☐	☐
☐	☐	☐
☐	☐	☐

WEEK:

Extras

1

2

3

4

5

6

Grades

★ Set aside an hour of unstructured outdoor playtime every day. This "green hour" can help reduce stress, improve concentration, and boost creative thinking—plus, it's fun!

	SUBJECT	GRADE
1		
2		
3		
4		
5		
6		

GRADES

WEEK

	MONDAY	TUESDAY	WEDNESDAY
1	☐	☐	☐
	☐	☐	☐
	☐	☐	☐
	☐	☐	☐
	☐	☐	☐
	☐	☐	☐
2	☐	☐	☐
	☐	☐	☐
	☐	☐	☐
	☐	☐	☐
	☐	☐	☐
	☐	☐	☐
3	☐	☐	☐
	☐	☐	☐
	☐	☐	☐
	☐	☐	☐
	☐	☐	☐
	☐	☐	☐
4	☐	☐	☐
	☐	☐	☐
	☐	☐	☐
	☐	☐	☐
	☐	☐	☐
	☐	☐	☐
5	☐	☐	☐
	☐	☐	☐
	☐	☐	☐
	☐	☐	☐
	☐	☐	☐
	☐	☐	☐
6	☐	☐	☐
	☐	☐	☐
	☐	☐	☐
	☐	☐	☐
	☐	☐	☐
	☐	☐	☐

WEEK:

Our knitting the net of subjects makes a sort of hammock: though it has holes, it will uplift and support its owner. While we knit, the children fill in the holes. By means of self-education, they acquire genuine, long-lasting knowledge—the real stuff. —KAREN ANDREOLA

THURSDAY	FRIDAY	SAT / SUN
☐	☐	☐
☐	☐	☐
☐	☐	☐
☐	☐	☐
☐	☐	☐
☐	☐	☐
☐	☐	☐
☐	☐	☐
☐	☐	☐
☐	☐	☐
☐	☐	☐
☐	☐	☐
☐	☐	☐
☐	☐	☐
☐	☐	☐
☐	☐	☐
☐	☐	☐
☐	☐	☐
☐	☐	☐
☐	☐	☐
☐	☐	☐
☐	☐	☐
☐	☐	☐
☐	☐	☐
☐	☐	☐
☐	☐	☐
☐	☐	☐
☐	☐	☐
☐	☐	☐
☐	☐	☐
☐	☐	☐
☐	☐	☐
☐	☐	☐
☐	☐	☐
☐	☐	☐
☐	☐	☐

WEEK:

Extras

1

2

3

4

5

6

EXTRAS

Grades

We must be willing to be a beginner over and over again in order to live a full life. —JILL BADONSKY

	SUBJECT	GRADE
1		
2		
3		
4		
5		
6		

GRADES

WEEK

	MONDAY	TUESDAY	WEDNESDAY
1	☐ ☐ ☐ ☐ ☐ ☐	☐ ☐ ☐ ☐ ☐ ☐	☐ ☐ ☐ ☐ ☐ ☐
2	☐ ☐ ☐ ☐ ☐ ☐	☐ ☐ ☐ ☐ ☐ ☐	☐ ☐ ☐ ☐ ☐ ☐
3	☐ ☐ ☐ ☐ ☐ ☐	☐ ☐ ☐ ☐ ☐ ☐	☐ ☐ ☐ ☐ ☐ ☐
4	☐ ☐ ☐ ☐ ☐ ☐	☐ ☐ ☐ ☐ ☐ ☐	☐ ☐ ☐ ☐ ☐ ☐
5	☐ ☐ ☐ ☐ ☐ ☐	☐ ☐ ☐ ☐ ☐ ☐	☐ ☐ ☐ ☐ ☐ ☐
6	☐ ☐ ☐ ☐ ☐ ☐	☐ ☐ ☐ ☐ ☐ ☐	☐ ☐ ☐ ☐ ☐ ☐

WEEK:

An education isn't how much you have committed to memory, or even how much you know. It's being able to differentiate between what you do know and what you don't. It's knowing where to go to find out what you need to know; and it's knowing how to use the information you get. —WILLIAM FEATHER

THURSDAY	FRIDAY	SAT / SUN
☐	☐	☐
☐	☐	☐
☐	☐	☐
☐	☐	☐
☐	☐	☐
☐	☐	☐
☐	☐	☐
☐	☐	☐
☐	☐	☐
☐	☐	☐
☐	☐	☐
☐	☐	☐
☐	☐	☐
☐	☐	☐
☐	☐	☐
☐	☐	☐
☐	☐	☐
☐	☐	☐
☐	☐	☐
☐	☐	☐
☐	☐	☐
☐	☐	☐
☐	☐	☐
☐	☐	☐
☐	☐	☐
☐	☐	☐
☐	☐	☐
☐	☐	☐
☐	☐	☐
☐	☐	☐
☐	☐	☐
☐	☐	☐
☐	☐	☐
☐	☐	☐
☐	☐	☐
☐	☐	☐

WEEK:

Extras

1

2

3

4

5

6

Grades

★ If your kids tend to drag their feet with post-activity clean-up or multiplication drills, try setting a timer to help speed them up. Working to beat the buzzer can make kids move a little faster.

	SUBJECT	GRADE
1		
2		
3		
4		
5		
6		

GRADES

WEEK

	MONDAY	TUESDAY	WEDNESDAY
1	☐ ☐ ☐ ☐ ☐ ☐	☐ ☐ ☐ ☐ ☐ ☐	☐ ☐ ☐ ☐ ☐ ☐
2	☐ ☐ ☐ ☐ ☐ ☐	☐ ☐ ☐ ☐ ☐ ☐	☐ ☐ ☐ ☐ ☐ ☐
3	☐ ☐ ☐ ☐ ☐ ☐	☐ ☐ ☐ ☐ ☐ ☐	☐ ☐ ☐ ☐ ☐ ☐
4	☐ ☐ ☐ ☐ ☐ ☐	☐ ☐ ☐ ☐ ☐ ☐	☐ ☐ ☐ ☐ ☐ ☐
5	☐ ☐ ☐ ☐ ☐ ☐	☐ ☐ ☐ ☐ ☐ ☐	☐ ☐ ☐ ☐ ☐ ☐
6	☐ ☐ ☐ ☐ ☐ ☐	☐ ☐ ☐ ☐ ☐ ☐	☐ ☐ ☐ ☐ ☐ ☐

★ If your child needs help growing her attention span, make time for games, like Simon Says, Freeze Dance, the Farmer in the Dell, or Red Light-Green Light. These fun games are effective ways to practice paying attention.

THURSDAY	FRIDAY	SAT / SUN
☐	☐	☐
☐	☐	☐
☐	☐	☐
☐	☐	☐
☐	☐	☐
☐	☐	☐
☐	☐	☐
☐	☐	☐
☐	☐	☐
☐	☐	☐
☐	☐	☐
☐	☐	☐
☐	☐	☐
☐	☐	☐
☐	☐	☐
☐	☐	☐
☐	☐	☐
☐	☐	☐
☐	☐	☐
☐	☐	☐
☐	☐	☐
☐	☐	☐
☐	☐	☐
☐	☐	☐
☐	☐	☐
☐	☐	☐
☐	☐	☐
☐	☐	☐
☐	☐	☐
☐	☐	☐
☐	☐	☐
☐	☐	☐
☐	☐	☐
☐	☐	☐
☐	☐	☐
☐	☐	☐

WEEK:

Extras

1

2

3

4

5

6

EXTRAS

Grades

You don't learn to walk by following rules. You learn by doing, and by falling over. —RICHARD BRANSON

	SUBJECT	GRADE
1		
2		
3		
4		
5		
6		

GRADES

WEEK

	MONDAY	TUESDAY	WEDNESDAY
1	☐	☐	☐
	☐	☐	☐
	☐	☐	☐
	☐	☐	☐
	☐	☐	☐
	☐	☐	☐
2	☐	☐	☐
	☐	☐	☐
	☐	☐	☐
	☐	☐	☐
	☐	☐	☐
	☐	☐	☐
3	☐	☐	☐
	☐	☐	☐
	☐	☐	☐
	☐	☐	☐
	☐	☐	☐
	☐	☐	☐
4	☐	☐	☐
	☐	☐	☐
	☐	☐	☐
	☐	☐	☐
	☐	☐	☐
	☐	☐	☐
5	☐	☐	☐
	☐	☐	☐
	☐	☐	☐
	☐	☐	☐
	☐	☐	☐
	☐	☐	☐
6	☐	☐	☐
	☐	☐	☐
	☐	☐	☐
	☐	☐	☐
	☐	☐	☐
	☐	☐	☐

WEEK:

If a child is to keep alive his inborn sense of wonder, he needs the companionship of at least one adult who can share it, rediscovering with him the joy, excitement, and mystery of the world we live in. —RACHEL CARSON

THURSDAY	FRIDAY	SAT / SUN
☐	☐	☐
☐	☐	☐
☐	☐	☐
☐	☐	☐
☐	☐	☐
☐	☐	☐
☐	☐	☐
☐	☐	☐
☐	☐	☐
☐	☐	☐
☐	☐	☐
☐	☐	☐
☐	☐	☐
☐	☐	☐
☐	☐	☐
☐	☐	☐
☐	☐	☐
☐	☐	☐
☐	☐	☐
☐	☐	☐
☐	☐	☐
☐	☐	☐
☐	☐	☐
☐	☐	☐
☐	☐	☐
☐	☐	☐
☐	☐	☐
☐	☐	☐
☐	☐	☐
☐	☐	☐
☐	☐	☐
☐	☐	☐
☐	☐	☐
☐	☐	☐
☐	☐	☐
☐	☐	☐

WEEK:

Extras

1

2

3

4

5

6

EXTRAS

Grades

★ Choose one word to focus on each year. Maybe it's *curiosity* or *passion* or *integrity*—whatever it is, use it as a touchstone to keep you connected to your bigger goals while focusing on everyday tasks.

	SUBJECT	GRADE
1		
2		
3		
4		
5		
6		

GRADES

WEEK

	MONDAY	TUESDAY	WEDNESDAY
1	☐ ☐ ☐ ☐ ☐ ☐	☐ ☐ ☐ ☐ ☐ ☐	☐ ☐ ☐ ☐ ☐ ☐
2	☐ ☐ ☐ ☐ ☐ ☐	☐ ☐ ☐ ☐ ☐ ☐	☐ ☐ ☐ ☐ ☐ ☐
3	☐ ☐ ☐ ☐ ☐ ☐	☐ ☐ ☐ ☐ ☐ ☐	☐ ☐ ☐ ☐ ☐ ☐
4	☐ ☐ ☐ ☐ ☐ ☐	☐ ☐ ☐ ☐ ☐ ☐	☐ ☐ ☐ ☐ ☐ ☐
5	☐ ☐ ☐ ☐ ☐ ☐	☐ ☐ ☐ ☐ ☐ ☐	☐ ☐ ☐ ☐ ☐ ☐
6	☐ ☐ ☐ ☐ ☐ ☐	☐ ☐ ☐ ☐ ☐ ☐	☐ ☐ ☐ ☐ ☐ ☐

WEEK:

★ Make getting a good night's sleep a priority for your students—whether that means rolling back bedtime or starting a little later in the morning. Good sleep habits can make students more alert and effective, and you'll have more patience and better focus if you're getting enough sleep, too.

THURSDAY	FRIDAY	SAT / SUN
☐	☐	☐
☐	☐	☐
☐	☐	☐
☐	☐	☐
☐	☐	☐
☐	☐	☐
☐	☐	☐
☐	☐	☐
☐	☐	☐
☐	☐	☐
☐	☐	☐
☐	☐	☐
☐	☐	☐
☐	☐	☐
☐	☐	☐
☐	☐	☐
☐	☐	☐
☐	☐	☐
☐	☐	☐
☐	☐	☐
☐	☐	☐
☐	☐	☐
☐	☐	☐
☐	☐	☐
☐	☐	☐
☐	☐	☐
☐	☐	☐
☐	☐	☐
☐	☐	☐
☐	☐	☐
☐	☐	☐
☐	☐	☐
☐	☐	☐
☐	☐	☐
☐	☐	☐
☐	☐	☐

WEEK:

Extras

1	2

3	4

5	6

EXTRAS

Grades

I'm always ready to learn, although I do not always like being taught. —WINSTON CHURCHILL

	SUBJECT	GRADE
1		
2		
3		
4		
5		
6		

WEEK

	MONDAY	TUESDAY	WEDNESDAY
1	☐ ☐ ☐ ☐ ☐ ☐	☐ ☐ ☐ ☐ ☐ ☐	☐ ☐ ☐ ☐ ☐ ☐
2	☐ ☐ ☐ ☐ ☐ ☐	☐ ☐ ☐ ☐ ☐ ☐	☐ ☐ ☐ ☐ ☐ ☐
3	☐ ☐ ☐ ☐ ☐ ☐	☐ ☐ ☐ ☐ ☐ ☐	☐ ☐ ☐ ☐ ☐ ☐
4	☐ ☐ ☐ ☐ ☐ ☐	☐ ☐ ☐ ☐ ☐ ☐	☐ ☐ ☐ ☐ ☐ ☐
5	☐ ☐ ☐ ☐ ☐ ☐	☐ ☐ ☐ ☐ ☐ ☐	☐ ☐ ☐ ☐ ☐ ☐
6	☐ ☐ ☐ ☐ ☐ ☐	☐ ☐ ☐ ☐ ☐ ☐	☐ ☐ ☐ ☐ ☐ ☐

WEEK:

★ Remind kids to do simple short-term tasks such as finding their library books, checking their addition, or putting away their school supplies after a lesson by making a paper reminder bracelet that they can tear off when the task is complete.

THURSDAY	FRIDAY	SAT / SUN
☐	☐	☐
☐	☐	☐
☐	☐	☐
☐	☐	☐
☐	☐	☐
☐	☐	☐
☐	☐	☐
☐	☐	☐
☐	☐	☐
☐	☐	☐
☐	☐	☐
☐	☐	☐
☐	☐	☐
☐	☐	☐
☐	☐	☐
☐	☐	☐
☐	☐	☐
☐	☐	☐
☐	☐	☐
☐	☐	☐
☐	☐	☐
☐	☐	☐
☐	☐	☐
☐	☐	☐
☐	☐	☐
☐	☐	☐
☐	☐	☐
☐	☐	☐
☐	☐	☐
☐	☐	☐
☐	☐	☐
☐	☐	☐
☐	☐	☐
☐	☐	☐
☐	☐	☐
☐	☐	☐

WEEK:

Extras

1

2

3

4

5

6

EXTRAS

Grades

★ Let your kids be your guide when you're evaluating how your homeschool is working. If things are working, great! If not, look for ways to change things for the better.

	SUBJECT	GRADE
1		
2		
3		
4		
5		
6		

GRADES

WEEK

	MONDAY	TUESDAY	WEDNESDAY
1	☐	☐	☐
	☐	☐	☐
	☐	☐	☐
	☐	☐	☐
	☐	☐	☐
	☐	☐	☐
2	☐	☐	☐
	☐	☐	☐
	☐	☐	☐
	☐	☐	☐
	☐	☐	☐
	☐	☐	☐
3	☐	☐	☐
	☐	☐	☐
	☐	☐	☐
	☐	☐	☐
	☐	☐	☐
	☐	☐	☐
4	☐	☐	☐
	☐	☐	☐
	☐	☐	☐
	☐	☐	☐
	☐	☐	☐
	☐	☐	☐
5	☐	☐	☐
	☐	☐	☐
	☐	☐	☐
	☐	☐	☐
	☐	☐	☐
	☐	☐	☐
6	☐	☐	☐
	☐	☐	☐
	☐	☐	☐
	☐	☐	☐
	☐	☐	☐
	☐	☐	☐

★ Kids learn best when they feel that what they're learning has a purpose. Before you dive into a subject, have an in-depth, thoughtful conversation with your child about why it matters. ("Because it shows up on the SAT" doesn't work unless the SAT is a big piece of your child's future goals.)

THURSDAY	FRIDAY	SAT / SUN
☐	☐	☐
☐	☐	☐
☐	☐	☐
☐	☐	☐
☐	☐	☐
☐	☐	☐
☐	☐	☐
☐	☐	☐
☐	☐	☐
☐	☐	☐
☐	☐	☐
☐	☐	☐
☐	☐	☐
☐	☐	☐
☐	☐	☐
☐	☐	☐
☐	☐	☐
☐	☐	☐
☐	☐	☐
☐	☐	☐
☐	☐	☐
☐	☐	☐
☐	☐	☐
☐	☐	☐
☐	☐	☐
☐	☐	☐
☐	☐	☐
☐	☐	☐
☐	☐	☐
☐	☐	☐
☐	☐	☐
☐	☐	☐
☐	☐	☐
☐	☐	☐
☐	☐	☐
☐	☐	☐

WEEK:

Extras

1

2

3

4

5

6

EXTRAS

Grades

Getting things done is not always what is most important. There is value in allowing others to learn, even if the task is not accomplished as quickly, efficiently, or effectively. —R.D. CLYDE

	SUBJECT	GRADE
1		
2		
3		
4		
5		
6		

GRADES

WEEK

	MONDAY	TUESDAY	WEDNESDAY
1			
2			
3			
4			
5			
6			

WEEK:

★ On a great homeschool day when you're feeling happy and successful, write a message to yourself to read the next time you're having a not-so-great day. Think about the words you need to hear when you snap at your child over a math lesson or have a major student meltdown that pushes all your buttons. Keep this note handy for times when you need a reminder that you're doing the right thing, even if it hasn't been a great week.

THURSDAY	FRIDAY	SAT / SUN
☐	☐	☐
☐	☐	☐
☐	☐	☐
☐	☐	☐
☐	☐	☐
☐	☐	☐
☐	☐	☐
☐	☐	☐
☐	☐	☐
☐	☐	☐
☐	☐	☐
☐	☐	☐
☐	☐	☐
☐	☐	☐
☐	☐	☐
☐	☐	☐
☐	☐	☐
☐	☐	☐
☐	☐	☐
☐	☐	☐
☐	☐	☐
☐	☐	☐
☐	☐	☐
☐	☐	☐
☐	☐	☐
☐	☐	☐
☐	☐	☐
☐	☐	☐
☐	☐	☐
☐	☐	☐
☐	☐	☐
☐	☐	☐
☐	☐	☐
☐	☐	☐
☐	☐	☐
☐	☐	☐

WEEK:

Extras

1

2

3

4

5

6

EXTRAS

Grades

Every student can learn. Just not on the same day or in the same way. —GEORGE EVANS

	SUBJECT	GRADE
1		
2		
3		
4		
5		
6		

GRADES

WEEK

WEEK:

	MONDAY	TUESDAY	WEDNESDAY
1	☐ ☐ ☐ ☐ ☐ ☐	☐ ☐ ☐ ☐ ☐ ☐	☐ ☐ ☐ ☐ ☐ ☐
2	☐ ☐ ☐ ☐ ☐ ☐	☐ ☐ ☐ ☐ ☐ ☐	☐ ☐ ☐ ☐ ☐ ☐
3	☐ ☐ ☐ ☐ ☐ ☐	☐ ☐ ☐ ☐ ☐ ☐	☐ ☐ ☐ ☐ ☐ ☐
4	☐ ☐ ☐ ☐ ☐ ☐	☐ ☐ ☐ ☐ ☐ ☐	☐ ☐ ☐ ☐ ☐ ☐
5	☐ ☐ ☐ ☐ ☐ ☐	☐ ☐ ☐ ☐ ☐ ☐	☐ ☐ ☐ ☐ ☐ ☐
6	☐ ☐ ☐ ☐ ☐ ☐	☐ ☐ ☐ ☐ ☐ ☐	☐ ☐ ☐ ☐ ☐ ☐

It does not matter how slowly you go as long as you do not stop. —CONFUCIUS

THURSDAY	FRIDAY	SAT / SUN
☐	☐	☐
☐	☐	☐
☐	☐	☐
☐	☐	☐
☐	☐	☐
☐	☐	☐
☐	☐	☐
☐	☐	☐
☐	☐	☐
☐	☐	☐
☐	☐	☐
☐	☐	☐
☐	☐	☐
☐	☐	☐
☐	☐	☐
☐	☐	☐
☐	☐	☐
☐	☐	☐
☐	☐	☐
☐	☐	☐
☐	☐	☐
☐	☐	☐
☐	☐	☐
☐	☐	☐
☐	☐	☐
☐	☐	☐
☐	☐	☐
☐	☐	☐
☐	☐	☐
☐	☐	☐
☐	☐	☐
☐	☐	☐
☐	☐	☐
☐	☐	☐
☐	☐	☐
☐	☐	☐

WEEK:

Extras

1

2

3

4

5

6

EXTRAS

Grades

You will not reap the fruit of individuality in your children if you clone their education. —MARILYN HOWSHALL

	SUBJECT	GRADE
1		
2		
3		
4		
5		
6		

GRADES

WEEK

	MONDAY	TUESDAY	WEDNESDAY
1	☐	☐	☐
	☐	☐	☐
	☐	☐	☐
	☐	☐	☐
	☐	☐	☐
	☐	☐	☐
2	☐	☐	☐
	☐	☐	☐
	☐	☐	☐
	☐	☐	☐
	☐	☐	☐
	☐	☐	☐
3	☐	☐	☐
	☐	☐	☐
	☐	☐	☐
	☐	☐	☐
	☐	☐	☐
	☐	☐	☐
4	☐	☐	☐
	☐	☐	☐
	☐	☐	☐
	☐	☐	☐
	☐	☐	☐
	☐	☐	☐
5	☐	☐	☐
	☐	☐	☐
	☐	☐	☐
	☐	☐	☐
	☐	☐	☐
	☐	☐	☐
6	☐	☐	☐
	☐	☐	☐
	☐	☐	☐
	☐	☐	☐
	☐	☐	☐
	☐	☐	☐

★ Count playtime as school time. Your child may be pretending to be a chef, building worlds in Minecraft, or just watching an anthill in the backyard, but they're learning while they're doing it. Let go of the need to make "school time" and let your child lead you in the direction he wants to learn.

THURSDAY	FRIDAY	SAT / SUN
☐	☐	☐
☐	☐	☐
☐	☐	☐
☐	☐	☐
☐	☐	☐
☐	☐	☐
☐	☐	☐
☐	☐	☐
☐	☐	☐
☐	☐	☐
☐	☐	☐
☐	☐	☐
☐	☐	☐
☐	☐	☐
☐	☐	☐
☐	☐	☐
☐	☐	☐
☐	☐	☐
☐	☐	☐
☐	☐	☐
☐	☐	☐
☐	☐	☐
☐	☐	☐
☐	☐	☐
☐	☐	☐
☐	☐	☐
☐	☐	☐
☐	☐	☐
☐	☐	☐
☐	☐	☐
☐	☐	☐
☐	☐	☐
☐	☐	☐
☐	☐	☐
☐	☐	☐
☐	☐	☐

WEEK:

Extras

1

2

3

4

5

6

EXTRAS

Grades

One is always a long way from solving a problem until one actually has the answer. —STEPHEN HAWKING

	SUBJECT	GRADE
1		
2		
3		
4		
5		
6		

WEEK

	MONDAY	TUESDAY	WEDNESDAY
1	☐ ☐ ☐ ☐ ☐ ☐	☐ ☐ ☐ ☐ ☐ ☐	☐ ☐ ☐ ☐ ☐ ☐
2	☐ ☐ ☐ ☐ ☐ ☐	☐ ☐ ☐ ☐ ☐ ☐	☐ ☐ ☐ ☐ ☐ ☐
3	☐ ☐ ☐ ☐ ☐ ☐	☐ ☐ ☐ ☐ ☐ ☐	☐ ☐ ☐ ☐ ☐ ☐
4	☐ ☐ ☐ ☐ ☐ ☐	☐ ☐ ☐ ☐ ☐ ☐	☐ ☐ ☐ ☐ ☐ ☐
5	☐ ☐ ☐ ☐ ☐ ☐	☐ ☐ ☐ ☐ ☐ ☐	☐ ☐ ☐ ☐ ☐ ☐
6	☐ ☐ ☐ ☐ ☐ ☐	☐ ☐ ☐ ☐ ☐ ☐	☐ ☐ ☐ ☐ ☐ ☐

WEEK:

★ When you're evaluating your homeschool parent success, make sure you're considering the week, not an individual day. Bad days happen, but they can disproportionately affect your homeschool confidence if you let them. Focusing on the week gives you a more balanced view of your homeschool's success.

THURSDAY	FRIDAY	SAT / SUN
☐	☐	☐
☐	☐	☐
☐	☐	☐
☐	☐	☐
☐	☐	☐
☐	☐	☐
☐	☐	☐
☐	☐	☐
☐	☐	☐
☐	☐	☐
☐	☐	☐
☐	☐	☐
☐	☐	☐
☐	☐	☐
☐	☐	☐
☐	☐	☐
☐	☐	☐
☐	☐	☐
☐	☐	☐
☐	☐	☐
☐	☐	☐
☐	☐	☐
☐	☐	☐
☐	☐	☐
☐	☐	☐
☐	☐	☐
☐	☐	☐
☐	☐	☐
☐	☐	☐
☐	☐	☐
☐	☐	☐
☐	☐	☐
☐	☐	☐
☐	☐	☐
☐	☐	☐
☐	☐	☐

WEEK:

Extras

1

2

3

4

5

6

EXTRAS

Grades

Nobody is bored when he is trying to make something that is beautiful or discover something that is true. —WILLIAM INGE

	SUBJECT	GRADE
1		
2		
3		
4		
5		
6		

GRADES

WEEK

	MONDAY	TUESDAY	WEDNESDAY
1	☐	☐	☐
	☐	☐	☐
	☐	☐	☐
	☐	☐	☐
	☐	☐	☐
	☐	☐	☐
2	☐	☐	☐
	☐	☐	☐
	☐	☐	☐
	☐	☐	☐
	☐	☐	☐
	☐	☐	☐
3	☐	☐	☐
	☐	☐	☐
	☐	☐	☐
	☐	☐	☐
	☐	☐	☐
	☐	☐	☐
4	☐	☐	☐
	☐	☐	☐
	☐	☐	☐
	☐	☐	☐
	☐	☐	☐
	☐	☐	☐
5	☐	☐	☐
	☐	☐	☐
	☐	☐	☐
	☐	☐	☐
	☐	☐	☐
	☐	☐	☐
6	☐	☐	☐
	☐	☐	☐
	☐	☐	☐
	☐	☐	☐
	☐	☐	☐
	☐	☐	☐

WEEK:

★ Everybody has gaps in their education, and your child will be no exception. There is no magical every-single-topic-gets-mastered curriculum. If you obsess over every possible knowledge gap, you'll make yourself—and your child—crazy. Have confidence in your ability to give your child a thorough education.

THURSDAY	FRIDAY	SAT / SUN
☐	☐	☐
☐	☐	☐
☐	☐	☐
☐	☐	☐
☐	☐	☐
☐	☐	☐
☐	☐	☐
☐	☐	☐
☐	☐	☐
☐	☐	☐
☐	☐	☐
☐	☐	☐
☐	☐	☐
☐	☐	☐
☐	☐	☐
☐	☐	☐
☐	☐	☐
☐	☐	☐
☐	☐	☐
☐	☐	☐
☐	☐	☐
☐	☐	☐
☐	☐	☐
☐	☐	☐
☐	☐	☐
☐	☐	☐
☐	☐	☐
☐	☐	☐
☐	☐	☐
☐	☐	☐
☐	☐	☐
☐	☐	☐
☐	☐	☐
☐	☐	☐
☐	☐	☐
☐	☐	☐

WEEK:

Extras

1

2

3

4

5

6

EXTRAS

Grades

★ Take advantage of "dead time," such as the hours you spend commuting to classes and activities or waiting in line, by downloading audiobooks or podcasts to listen to together.

	SUBJECT	GRADE
1		
2		
3		
4		
5		
6		

WEEK

	MONDAY	TUESDAY	WEDNESDAY
1	☐ ☐ ☐ ☐ ☐ ☐	☐ ☐ ☐ ☐ ☐ ☐	☐ ☐ ☐ ☐ ☐ ☐
2	☐ ☐ ☐ ☐ ☐ ☐	☐ ☐ ☐ ☐ ☐ ☐	☐ ☐ ☐ ☐ ☐ ☐
3	☐ ☐ ☐ ☐ ☐ ☐	☐ ☐ ☐ ☐ ☐ ☐	☐ ☐ ☐ ☐ ☐ ☐
4	☐ ☐ ☐ ☐ ☐ ☐	☐ ☐ ☐ ☐ ☐ ☐	☐ ☐ ☐ ☐ ☐ ☐
5	☐ ☐ ☐ ☐ ☐ ☐	☐ ☐ ☐ ☐ ☐ ☐	☐ ☐ ☐ ☐ ☐ ☐
6	☐ ☐ ☐ ☐ ☐ ☐	☐ ☐ ☐ ☐ ☐ ☐	☐ ☐ ☐ ☐ ☐ ☐

★ The key to keeping your homeschool organized is to spend about 10 minutes at the end of your school day tidying up your learning spaces and prepping for the next day. It may seem like a small project with minimal impact, but it can reduce long-term homeschool clutter sprawl in a big way.

THURSDAY	FRIDAY	SAT / SUN
☐	☐	☐
☐	☐	☐
☐	☐	☐
☐	☐	☐
☐	☐	☐
☐	☐	☐
☐	☐	☐
☐	☐	☐
☐	☐	☐
☐	☐	☐
☐	☐	☐
☐	☐	☐
☐	☐	☐
☐	☐	☐
☐	☐	☐
☐	☐	☐
☐	☐	☐
☐	☐	☐
☐	☐	☐
☐	☐	☐
☐	☐	☐
☐	☐	☐
☐	☐	☐
☐	☐	☐
☐	☐	☐
☐	☐	☐
☐	☐	☐
☐	☐	☐
☐	☐	☐
☐	☐	☐
☐	☐	☐
☐	☐	☐
☐	☐	☐
☐	☐	☐
☐	☐	☐
☐	☐	☐

WEEK:

Extras

1

2

3

4

5

6

EXTRAS

Grades

You can tell whether a man is clever by his answers.
You can tell whether a man is wise by his questions.
—NAGUIB MAHFOUZ

	SUBJECT	GRADE
1		
2		
3		
4		
5		
6		

GRADES

WEEK

	MONDAY	TUESDAY	WEDNESDAY
1	☐	☐	☐
	☐	☐	☐
	☐	☐	☐
	☐	☐	☐
	☐	☐	☐
	☐	☐	☐
2	☐	☐	☐
	☐	☐	☐
	☐	☐	☐
	☐	☐	☐
	☐	☐	☐
	☐	☐	☐
3	☐	☐	☐
	☐	☐	☐
	☐	☐	☐
	☐	☐	☐
	☐	☐	☐
	☐	☐	☐
4	☐	☐	☐
	☐	☐	☐
	☐	☐	☐
	☐	☐	☐
	☐	☐	☐
	☐	☐	☐
5	☐	☐	☐
	☐	☐	☐
	☐	☐	☐
	☐	☐	☐
	☐	☐	☐
	☐	☐	☐
6	☐	☐	☐
	☐	☐	☐
	☐	☐	☐
	☐	☐	☐
	☐	☐	☐
	☐	☐	☐

Children want to learn to the degree that they are unable to distinguish learning from fun. They keep this attitude until we adults convince them that learning is not fun. —GLENN DOMAN

THURSDAY	FRIDAY	SAT / SUN
☐	☐	☐
☐	☐	☐
☐	☐	☐
☐	☐	☐
☐	☐	☐
☐	☐	☐
☐	☐	☐
☐	☐	☐
☐	☐	☐
☐	☐	☐
☐	☐	☐
☐	☐	☐
☐	☐	☐
☐	☐	☐
☐	☐	☐
☐	☐	☐
☐	☐	☐
☐	☐	☐
☐	☐	☐
☐	☐	☐
☐	☐	☐
☐	☐	☐
☐	☐	☐
☐	☐	☐
☐	☐	☐
☐	☐	☐
☐	☐	☐
☐	☐	☐
☐	☐	☐
☐	☐	☐
☐	☐	☐
☐	☐	☐
☐	☐	☐
☐	☐	☐
☐	☐	☐
☐	☐	☐

WEEK:

Extras

1

2

3

4

5

6

EXTRAS

Grades

I think you learn more if you're laughing at the same time.
—MARY ANN SHAFFER

	SUBJECT	GRADE
1		
2		
3		
4		
5		
6		

GRADES

WEEK

	MONDAY	TUESDAY	WEDNESDAY
1	☐	☐	☐
	☐	☐	☐
	☐	☐	☐
	☐	☐	☐
	☐	☐	☐
	☐	☐	☐
2	☐	☐	☐
	☐	☐	☐
	☐	☐	☐
	☐	☐	☐
	☐	☐	☐
	☐	☐	☐
3	☐	☐	☐
	☐	☐	☐
	☐	☐	☐
	☐	☐	☐
	☐	☐	☐
	☐	☐	☐
4	☐	☐	☐
	☐	☐	☐
	☐	☐	☐
	☐	☐	☐
	☐	☐	☐
	☐	☐	☐
5	☐	☐	☐
	☐	☐	☐
	☐	☐	☐
	☐	☐	☐
	☐	☐	☐
	☐	☐	☐
6	☐	☐	☐
	☐	☐	☐
	☐	☐	☐
	☐	☐	☐
	☐	☐	☐
	☐	☐	☐

★ Don't assume that more means better. If you're enjoying 20 great minutes of history every day and slogging through class when you add more to it, let yourself enjoy the learning that's happening without trying to make it last longer.

THURSDAY	FRIDAY	SAT / SUN
☐	☐	☐
☐	☐	☐
☐	☐	☐
☐	☐	☐
☐	☐	☐
☐	☐	☐
☐	☐	☐
☐	☐	☐
☐	☐	☐
☐	☐	☐
☐	☐	☐
☐	☐	☐
☐	☐	☐
☐	☐	☐
☐	☐	☐
☐	☐	☐
☐	☐	☐
☐	☐	☐
☐	☐	☐
☐	☐	☐
☐	☐	☐
☐	☐	☐
☐	☐	☐
☐	☐	☐
☐	☐	☐
☐	☐	☐
☐	☐	☐
☐	☐	☐
☐	☐	☐
☐	☐	☐
☐	☐	☐
☐	☐	☐
☐	☐	☐
☐	☐	☐
☐	☐	☐
☐	☐	☐

WEEK:

Extras

1

2

3

4

5

6

Grades

★ Sometimes you want to be the best, but sometimes (Tuesday night dinner? Friday morning math?) just getting the job done counts as success. Give yourself permission to just be okay sometimes.

	SUBJECT	GRADE
1		
2		
3		
4		
5		
6		

GRADES

WEEK

	MONDAY	TUESDAY	WEDNESDAY
1	☐	☐	☐
	☐	☐	☐
	☐	☐	☐
	☐	☐	☐
	☐	☐	☐
	☐	☐	☐
2	☐	☐	☐
	☐	☐	☐
	☐	☐	☐
	☐	☐	☐
	☐	☐	☐
	☐	☐	☐
3	☐	☐	☐
	☐	☐	☐
	☐	☐	☐
	☐	☐	☐
	☐	☐	☐
	☐	☐	☐
4	☐	☐	☐
	☐	☐	☐
	☐	☐	☐
	☐	☐	☐
	☐	☐	☐
	☐	☐	☐
5	☐	☐	☐
	☐	☐	☐
	☐	☐	☐
	☐	☐	☐
	☐	☐	☐
	☐	☐	☐
6	☐	☐	☐
	☐	☐	☐
	☐	☐	☐
	☐	☐	☐
	☐	☐	☐
	☐	☐	☐

WEEK:

It is not so much what we are taught, but what we are surrounded by, that determines the course of our lives: the music and poetry and talk, the bright cocoon of life that is woven around us. —JULIE KELLER

THURSDAY	FRIDAY	SAT / SUN
☐	☐	☐
☐	☐	☐
☐	☐	☐
☐	☐	☐
☐	☐	☐
☐	☐	☐
☐	☐	☐
☐	☐	☐
☐	☐	☐
☐	☐	☐
☐	☐	☐
☐	☐	☐
☐	☐	☐
☐	☐	☐
☐	☐	☐
☐	☐	☐
☐	☐	☐
☐	☐	☐
☐	☐	☐
☐	☐	☐
☐	☐	☐
☐	☐	☐
☐	☐	☐
☐	☐	☐
☐	☐	☐
☐	☐	☐
☐	☐	☐
☐	☐	☐
☐	☐	☐
☐	☐	☐
☐	☐	☐
☐	☐	☐
☐	☐	☐
☐	☐	☐
☐	☐	☐
☐	☐	☐

WEEK:

Extras

1

2

3

4

5

6

EXTRAS

Grades

We need to move beyond the idea that an education is something provided for us, and toward the idea that an education is something that we create for ourselves.
—STEPHEN DOWNES

	SUBJECT	GRADE
1		
2		
3		
4		
5		
6		

GRADES

WEEK

	MONDAY	TUESDAY	WEDNESDAY
1	☐	☐	☐
	☐	☐	☐
	☐	☐	☐
	☐	☐	☐
	☐	☐	☐
	☐	☐	☐
2	☐	☐	☐
	☐	☐	☐
	☐	☐	☐
	☐	☐	☐
	☐	☐	☐
	☐	☐	☐
3	☐	☐	☐
	☐	☐	☐
	☐	☐	☐
	☐	☐	☐
	☐	☐	☐
	☐	☐	☐
4	☐	☐	☐
	☐	☐	☐
	☐	☐	☐
	☐	☐	☐
	☐	☐	☐
	☐	☐	☐
5	☐	☐	☐
	☐	☐	☐
	☐	☐	☐
	☐	☐	☐
	☐	☐	☐
	☐	☐	☐
6	☐	☐	☐
	☐	☐	☐
	☐	☐	☐
	☐	☐	☐
	☐	☐	☐
	☐	☐	☐

★ Don't be afraid to think outside the traditional school day. If you'd rather do science labs on weekends or reading together at bedtime, go right ahead. One of the great benefits of homeschooling is having the freedom to structure your day the way that works best for your family.

THURSDAY	FRIDAY	SAT / SUN
☐	☐	☐
☐	☐	☐
☐	☐	☐
☐	☐	☐
☐	☐	☐
☐	☐	☐
☐	☐	☐
☐	☐	☐
☐	☐	☐
☐	☐	☐
☐	☐	☐
☐	☐	☐
☐	☐	☐
☐	☐	☐
☐	☐	☐
☐	☐	☐
☐	☐	☐
☐	☐	☐
☐	☐	☐
☐	☐	☐
☐	☐	☐
☐	☐	☐
☐	☐	☐
☐	☐	☐
☐	☐	☐
☐	☐	☐
☐	☐	☐
☐	☐	☐
☐	☐	☐
☐	☐	☐
☐	☐	☐
☐	☐	☐
☐	☐	☐
☐	☐	☐
☐	☐	☐
☐	☐	☐

WEEK:

Extras

1

2

3

4

5

6

EXTRAS

Grades

★ If your kids are having trouble focusing as you shift subjects, consider a change of scenery. If you do your math at the kitchen table, move your read-aloud to the back porch or the couch.

	SUBJECT	GRADE
1		
2		
3		
4		
5		
6		

GRADES

WEEK

	MONDAY	TUESDAY	WEDNESDAY
1	☐	☐	☐
	☐	☐	☐
	☐	☐	☐
	☐	☐	☐
	☐	☐	☐
	☐	☐	☐
2	☐	☐	☐
	☐	☐	☐
	☐	☐	☐
	☐	☐	☐
	☐	☐	☐
	☐	☐	☐
3	☐	☐	☐
	☐	☐	☐
	☐	☐	☐
	☐	☐	☐
	☐	☐	☐
	☐	☐	☐
4	☐	☐	☐
	☐	☐	☐
	☐	☐	☐
	☐	☐	☐
	☐	☐	☐
	☐	☐	☐
5	☐	☐	☐
	☐	☐	☐
	☐	☐	☐
	☐	☐	☐
	☐	☐	☐
	☐	☐	☐
6	☐	☐	☐
	☐	☐	☐
	☐	☐	☐
	☐	☐	☐
	☐	☐	☐
	☐	☐	☐

★ Pause every once in a while to give yourself a pat on the back. Homeschooling is hard work, and it's easy to second-guess your decisions or beat yourself up when you're grumpy or ineffective one day. Wanting to improve is always a worthy goal, but don't forget to give yourself credit for everything you're doing right.

THURSDAY	FRIDAY	SAT / SUN
☐	☐	☐
☐	☐	☐
☐	☐	☐
☐	☐	☐
☐	☐	☐
☐	☐	☐
☐	☐	☐
☐	☐	☐
☐	☐	☐
☐	☐	☐
☐	☐	☐
☐	☐	☐
☐	☐	☐
☐	☐	☐
☐	☐	☐
☐	☐	☐
☐	☐	☐
☐	☐	☐
☐	☐	☐
☐	☐	☐
☐	☐	☐
☐	☐	☐
☐	☐	☐
☐	☐	☐
☐	☐	☐
☐	☐	☐
☐	☐	☐
☐	☐	☐
☐	☐	☐
☐	☐	☐
☐	☐	☐
☐	☐	☐
☐	☐	☐
☐	☐	☐
☐	☐	☐
☐	☐	☐

WEEK:

Extras

1

2

3

4

5

6

EXTRAS

Grades

I believe that what we become depends on what our fathers teach us at odd moments, when they aren't trying to teach us. We are formed by little scraps of wisdom. —UMBERTO ECO

	SUBJECT	GRADE
1		
2		
3		
4		
5		
6		

GRADES

WEEK

	MONDAY	TUESDAY	WEDNESDAY
1	☐	☐	☐
	☐	☐	☐
	☐	☐	☐
	☐	☐	☐
	☐	☐	☐
	☐	☐	☐
2	☐	☐	☐
	☐	☐	☐
	☐	☐	☐
	☐	☐	☐
	☐	☐	☐
	☐	☐	☐
3	☐	☐	☐
	☐	☐	☐
	☐	☐	☐
	☐	☐	☐
	☐	☐	☐
	☐	☐	☐
4	☐	☐	☐
	☐	☐	☐
	☐	☐	☐
	☐	☐	☐
	☐	☐	☐
	☐	☐	☐
5	☐	☐	☐
	☐	☐	☐
	☐	☐	☐
	☐	☐	☐
	☐	☐	☐
	☐	☐	☐
6	☐	☐	☐
	☐	☐	☐
	☐	☐	☐
	☐	☐	☐
	☐	☐	☐
	☐	☐	☐

★ When your child is struggling with something, resist the urge to jump right in and help. Instead, give your child a little space to figure things out on her own—and when you do offer to help, start by asking what she's already done to try to solve the problem.

THURSDAY	FRIDAY	SAT / SUN
☐	☐	☐
☐	☐	☐
☐	☐	☐
☐	☐	☐
☐	☐	☐
☐	☐	☐
☐	☐	☐
☐	☐	☐
☐	☐	☐
☐	☐	☐
☐	☐	☐
☐	☐	☐
☐	☐	☐
☐	☐	☐
☐	☐	☐
☐	☐	☐
☐	☐	☐
☐	☐	☐
☐	☐	☐
☐	☐	☐
☐	☐	☐
☐	☐	☐
☐	☐	☐
☐	☐	☐
☐	☐	☐
☐	☐	☐
☐	☐	☐
☐	☐	☐
☐	☐	☐
☐	☐	☐
☐	☐	☐
☐	☐	☐
☐	☐	☐
☐	☐	☐
☐	☐	☐
☐	☐	☐

Extras

1

2

3

4

5

6

EXTRAS

Grades

Treat people as if they were what they ought to be and you help them become what they are capable of becoming.
—JOHANN WOLFGANG VON GOETHE

	SUBJECT	GRADE
1		
2		
3		
4		
5		
6		

GRADES

WEEK

WEEK:

	MONDAY	TUESDAY	WEDNESDAY
1	☐	☐	☐
	☐	☐	☐
	☐	☐	☐
	☐	☐	☐
	☐	☐	☐
	☐	☐	☐
2	☐	☐	☐
	☐	☐	☐
	☐	☐	☐
	☐	☐	☐
	☐	☐	☐
	☐	☐	☐
3	☐	☐	☐
	☐	☐	☐
	☐	☐	☐
	☐	☐	☐
	☐	☐	☐
	☐	☐	☐
4	☐	☐	☐
	☐	☐	☐
	☐	☐	☐
	☐	☐	☐
	☐	☐	☐
	☐	☐	☐
5	☐	☐	☐
	☐	☐	☐
	☐	☐	☐
	☐	☐	☐
	☐	☐	☐
	☐	☐	☐
6	☐	☐	☐
	☐	☐	☐
	☐	☐	☐
	☐	☐	☐
	☐	☐	☐
	☐	☐	☐

★ The best way to help your children become life learners is to set an example by becoming a life learner yourself. Pick your own projects and let your kids know what you're doing to pursue them—whether it's reading a book, watching an online video, or taking a class. (Bonus: You get to learn more about something you're interested in!)

THURSDAY	FRIDAY	SAT / SUN
☐	☐	☐
☐	☐	☐
☐	☐	☐
☐	☐	☐
☐	☐	☐
☐	☐	☐
☐	☐	☐
☐	☐	☐
☐	☐	☐
☐	☐	☐
☐	☐	☐
☐	☐	☐
☐	☐	☐
☐	☐	☐
☐	☐	☐
☐	☐	☐
☐	☐	☐
☐	☐	☐
☐	☐	☐
☐	☐	☐
☐	☐	☐
☐	☐	☐
☐	☐	☐
☐	☐	☐
☐	☐	☐
☐	☐	☐
☐	☐	☐
☐	☐	☐
☐	☐	☐
☐	☐	☐
☐	☐	☐
☐	☐	☐
☐	☐	☐
☐	☐	☐
☐	☐	☐
☐	☐	☐

WEEK:

Extras

1

2

3

4

5

6

EXTRAS

Grades

★ Life might get crazy and throw your homeschool plans for a loop at times. When that happens, remind yourself that you're not working on a strict timeline—you can take a break and pick back up when you're ready.

	SUBJECT	GRADE
1		
2		
3		
4		
5		
6		

WEEK

	MONDAY	TUESDAY	WEDNESDAY
1	☐	☐	☐
	☐	☐	☐
	☐	☐	☐
	☐	☐	☐
	☐	☐	☐
	☐	☐	☐
2	☐	☐	☐
	☐	☐	☐
	☐	☐	☐
	☐	☐	☐
	☐	☐	☐
	☐	☐	☐
3	☐	☐	☐
	☐	☐	☐
	☐	☐	☐
	☐	☐	☐
	☐	☐	☐
	☐	☐	☐
4	☐	☐	☐
	☐	☐	☐
	☐	☐	☐
	☐	☐	☐
	☐	☐	☐
	☐	☐	☐
5	☐	☐	☐
	☐	☐	☐
	☐	☐	☐
	☐	☐	☐
	☐	☐	☐
	☐	☐	☐
6	☐	☐	☐
	☐	☐	☐
	☐	☐	☐
	☐	☐	☐
	☐	☐	☐
	☐	☐	☐

★ If your family's reading enthusiasm is lagging, launch a family read-a-thon with an ambitious "pages read" goal. (Set a family goal if you want to avoid individual competition between kids.) With a fun reward, like a trip to a water park or tickets to an upcoming movie, this project can boost everyone's reading excitement.

THURSDAY	FRIDAY	SAT / SUN
☐	☐	☐
☐	☐	☐
☐	☐	☐
☐	☐	☐
☐	☐	☐
☐	☐	☐
☐	☐	☐
☐	☐	☐
☐	☐	☐
☐	☐	☐
☐	☐	☐
☐	☐	☐
☐	☐	☐
☐	☐	☐
☐	☐	☐
☐	☐	☐
☐	☐	☐
☐	☐	☐
☐	☐	☐
☐	☐	☐
☐	☐	☐
☐	☐	☐
☐	☐	☐
☐	☐	☐
☐	☐	☐
☐	☐	☐
☐	☐	☐
☐	☐	☐
☐	☐	☐
☐	☐	☐
☐	☐	☐
☐	☐	☐
☐	☐	☐
☐	☐	☐
☐	☐	☐
☐	☐	☐

Extras

1

2

3

4

5

6

EXTRAS

Grades

The greatest sign of success for a teacher is to be able to say, "The children are now working as if I did not exist."
—MARIA MONTESSORI

	SUBJECT	GRADE
1		
2		
3		
4		
5		
6		

WEEK

	MONDAY	TUESDAY	WEDNESDAY
1	☐	☐	☐
	☐	☐	☐
	☐	☐	☐
	☐	☐	☐
	☐	☐	☐
	☐	☐	☐
2	☐	☐	☐
	☐	☐	☐
	☐	☐	☐
	☐	☐	☐
	☐	☐	☐
	☐	☐	☐
3	☐	☐	☐
	☐	☐	☐
	☐	☐	☐
	☐	☐	☐
	☐	☐	☐
	☐	☐	☐
4	☐	☐	☐
	☐	☐	☐
	☐	☐	☐
	☐	☐	☐
	☐	☐	☐
	☐	☐	☐
5	☐	☐	☐
	☐	☐	☐
	☐	☐	☐
	☐	☐	☐
	☐	☐	☐
	☐	☐	☐
6	☐	☐	☐
	☐	☐	☐
	☐	☐	☐
	☐	☐	☐
	☐	☐	☐
	☐	☐	☐

★ Our secret weapon for a really tough week: Go backward. Start the day with dessert, pajamas, and a bedtime story, and work your way back to breakfast for dinner. It's weird and wacky and somehow just the right thing to get everyone in a happier mood.

THURSDAY	FRIDAY	SAT / SUN
☐	☐	☐
☐	☐	☐
☐	☐	☐
☐	☐	☐
☐	☐	☐
☐	☐	☐
☐	☐	☐
☐	☐	☐
☐	☐	☐
☐	☐	☐
☐	☐	☐
☐	☐	☐
☐	☐	☐
☐	☐	☐
☐	☐	☐
☐	☐	☐
☐	☐	☐
☐	☐	☐
☐	☐	☐
☐	☐	☐
☐	☐	☐
☐	☐	☐
☐	☐	☐
☐	☐	☐
☐	☐	☐
☐	☐	☐
☐	☐	☐
☐	☐	☐
☐	☐	☐
☐	☐	☐
☐	☐	☐
☐	☐	☐
☐	☐	☐
☐	☐	☐
☐	☐	☐
☐	☐	☐

WEEK:

Extras

1

2

3

4

5

6

EXTRAS

Grades

The purpose of life is to be defeated by greater and greater things. —RAINER MARIA RILKE

	SUBJECT	GRADE
1		
2		
3		
4		
5		
6		

GRADES

WEEK

	MONDAY	TUESDAY	WEDNESDAY
1	☐	☐	☐
	☐	☐	☐
	☐	☐	☐
	☐	☐	☐
	☐	☐	☐
	☐	☐	☐
2	☐	☐	☐
	☐	☐	☐
	☐	☐	☐
	☐	☐	☐
	☐	☐	☐
	☐	☐	☐
3	☐	☐	☐
	☐	☐	☐
	☐	☐	☐
	☐	☐	☐
	☐	☐	☐
	☐	☐	☐
4	☐	☐	☐
	☐	☐	☐
	☐	☐	☐
	☐	☐	☐
	☐	☐	☐
	☐	☐	☐
5	☐	☐	☐
	☐	☐	☐
	☐	☐	☐
	☐	☐	☐
	☐	☐	☐
	☐	☐	☐
6	☐	☐	☐
	☐	☐	☐
	☐	☐	☐
	☐	☐	☐
	☐	☐	☐
	☐	☐	☐

The reasonable man adapts himself to the world: the unreasonable one persists in trying to adapt the world to himself. Therefore all progress depends on the unreasonable man. —**GEORGE BERNARD SHAW**

THURSDAY	FRIDAY	SAT / SUN
☐	☐	☐
☐	☐	☐
☐	☐	☐
☐	☐	☐
☐	☐	☐
☐	☐	☐
☐	☐	☐
☐	☐	☐
☐	☐	☐
☐	☐	☐
☐	☐	☐
☐	☐	☐
☐	☐	☐
☐	☐	☐
☐	☐	☐
☐	☐	☐
☐	☐	☐
☐	☐	☐
☐	☐	☐
☐	☐	☐
☐	☐	☐
☐	☐	☐
☐	☐	☐
☐	☐	☐
☐	☐	☐
☐	☐	☐
☐	☐	☐
☐	☐	☐
☐	☐	☐
☐	☐	☐
☐	☐	☐
☐	☐	☐
☐	☐	☐
☐	☐	☐
☐	☐	☐
☐	☐	☐

Extras

1

2

3

4

5

6

EXTRAS

Grades

Do what you can, with what you have, where you are.
—THEODORE ROOSEVELT

	SUBJECT	GRADE
1		
2		
3		
4		
5		
6		

WEEK

	MONDAY	TUESDAY	WEDNESDAY
1	☐	☐	☐
	☐	☐	☐
	☐	☐	☐
	☐	☐	☐
	☐	☐	☐
	☐	☐	☐
2	☐	☐	☐
	☐	☐	☐
	☐	☐	☐
	☐	☐	☐
	☐	☐	☐
	☐	☐	☐
3	☐	☐	☐
	☐	☐	☐
	☐	☐	☐
	☐	☐	☐
	☐	☐	☐
	☐	☐	☐
4	☐	☐	☐
	☐	☐	☐
	☐	☐	☐
	☐	☐	☐
	☐	☐	☐
	☐	☐	☐
5	☐	☐	☐
	☐	☐	☐
	☐	☐	☐
	☐	☐	☐
	☐	☐	☐
	☐	☐	☐
6	☐	☐	☐
	☐	☐	☐
	☐	☐	☐
	☐	☐	☐
	☐	☐	☐
	☐	☐	☐

If a man does not keep pace with his companions, perhaps it is because he hears a different drummer. Let him step to the music which he hears, however measured or far away. —HENRY DAVID THOREAU

THURSDAY	FRIDAY	SAT / SUN
☐	☐	☐
☐	☐	☐
☐	☐	☐
☐	☐	☐
☐	☐	☐
☐	☐	☐
☐	☐	☐
☐	☐	☐
☐	☐	☐
☐	☐	☐
☐	☐	☐
☐	☐	☐
☐	☐	☐
☐	☐	☐
☐	☐	☐
☐	☐	☐
☐	☐	☐
☐	☐	☐
☐	☐	☐
☐	☐	☐
☐	☐	☐
☐	☐	☐
☐	☐	☐
☐	☐	☐
☐	☐	☐
☐	☐	☐
☐	☐	☐
☐	☐	☐
☐	☐	☐
☐	☐	☐
☐	☐	☐
☐	☐	☐
☐	☐	☐
☐	☐	☐
☐	☐	☐
☐	☐	☐

Extras

1

2

3

4

5

6

EXTRAS

Grades

Start by doing what's necessary; then do what's possible; and suddenly you are doing the impossible. —FRANCIS OF ASSISI

	SUBJECT	GRADE
1		
2		
3		
4		
5		
6		

GRADES

WEEK

	MONDAY	TUESDAY	WEDNESDAY
1	☐	☐	☐
	☐	☐	☐
	☐	☐	☐
	☐	☐	☐
	☐	☐	☐
	☐	☐	☐
2	☐	☐	☐
	☐	☐	☐
	☐	☐	☐
	☐	☐	☐
	☐	☐	☐
	☐	☐	☐
3	☐	☐	☐
	☐	☐	☐
	☐	☐	☐
	☐	☐	☐
	☐	☐	☐
	☐	☐	☐
4	☐	☐	☐
	☐	☐	☐
	☐	☐	☐
	☐	☐	☐
	☐	☐	☐
	☐	☐	☐
5	☐	☐	☐
	☐	☐	☐
	☐	☐	☐
	☐	☐	☐
	☐	☐	☐
	☐	☐	☐
6	☐	☐	☐
	☐	☐	☐
	☐	☐	☐
	☐	☐	☐
	☐	☐	☐
	☐	☐	☐

★ Fill an A-to-Z accordion file (either a paper or a digital version) with subject-sorted ideas for unit studies, curricula, related books, and anything else you find interesting. Then, when you're ready to explore that subject, you already have a starter list of resources.

THURSDAY	FRIDAY	SAT / SUN
☐	☐	☐
☐	☐	☐
☐	☐	☐
☐	☐	☐
☐	☐	☐
☐	☐	☐
☐	☐	☐
☐	☐	☐
☐	☐	☐
☐	☐	☐
☐	☐	☐
☐	☐	☐
☐	☐	☐
☐	☐	☐
☐	☐	☐
☐	☐	☐
☐	☐	☐
☐	☐	☐
☐	☐	☐
☐	☐	☐
☐	☐	☐
☐	☐	☐
☐	☐	☐
☐	☐	☐
☐	☐	☐
☐	☐	☐
☐	☐	☐
☐	☐	☐
☐	☐	☐
☐	☐	☐
☐	☐	☐
☐	☐	☐
☐	☐	☐
☐	☐	☐
☐	☐	☐
☐	☐	☐

WEEK:

Extras

1

2

3

4

5

6

EXTRAS

Grades

When you make the finding yourself—even if you are the last person on Earth to see the light—you will never forget it.
—CARL SAGAN

	SUBJECT	GRADE
1		
2		
3		
4		
5		
6		

WEEK

WEEK:

	MONDAY	TUESDAY	WEDNESDAY
1	☐ ☐ ☐ ☐ ☐ ☐	☐ ☐ ☐ ☐ ☐ ☐	☐ ☐ ☐ ☐ ☐ ☐
2	☐ ☐ ☐ ☐ ☐ ☐	☐ ☐ ☐ ☐ ☐ ☐	☐ ☐ ☐ ☐ ☐ ☐
3	☐ ☐ ☐ ☐ ☐ ☐	☐ ☐ ☐ ☐ ☐ ☐	☐ ☐ ☐ ☐ ☐ ☐
4	☐ ☐ ☐ ☐ ☐ ☐	☐ ☐ ☐ ☐ ☐ ☐	☐ ☐ ☐ ☐ ☐ ☐
5	☐ ☐ ☐ ☐ ☐ ☐	☐ ☐ ☐ ☐ ☐ ☐	☐ ☐ ☐ ☐ ☐ ☐
6	☐ ☐ ☐ ☐ ☐ ☐	☐ ☐ ☐ ☐ ☐ ☐	☐ ☐ ☐ ☐ ☐ ☐

If uncertainty is unacceptable to you, it turns into fear. If it is perfectly acceptable, it turns into aliveness, alertness, and creativity. —ECKHART TOLLE

THURSDAY	FRIDAY	SAT / SUN
☐	☐	☐
☐	☐	☐
☐	☐	☐
☐	☐	☐
☐	☐	☐
☐	☐	☐
☐	☐	☐
☐	☐	☐
☐	☐	☐
☐	☐	☐
☐	☐	☐
☐	☐	☐
☐	☐	☐
☐	☐	☐
☐	☐	☐
☐	☐	☐
☐	☐	☐
☐	☐	☐
☐	☐	☐
☐	☐	☐
☐	☐	☐
☐	☐	☐
☐	☐	☐
☐	☐	☐
☐	☐	☐
☐	☐	☐
☐	☐	☐
☐	☐	☐
☐	☐	☐
☐	☐	☐
☐	☐	☐
☐	☐	☐
☐	☐	☐
☐	☐	☐
☐	☐	☐
☐	☐	☐

WEEK:

Extras

1

2

3

4

5

6

EXTRAS

Grades

We spend the first year of a child's life teaching it to walk and talk and the rest of its life to shut up and sit down. There's something wrong there. —NEIL DEGRASSE TYSON

	SUBJECT	GRADE
1		
2		
3		
4		
5		
6		

WEEK

	MONDAY	TUESDAY	WEDNESDAY
1	☐	☐	☐
	☐	☐	☐
	☐	☐	☐
	☐	☐	☐
	☐	☐	☐
	☐	☐	☐
2	☐	☐	☐
	☐	☐	☐
	☐	☐	☐
	☐	☐	☐
	☐	☐	☐
	☐	☐	☐
3	☐	☐	☐
	☐	☐	☐
	☐	☐	☐
	☐	☐	☐
	☐	☐	☐
	☐	☐	☐
4	☐	☐	☐
	☐	☐	☐
	☐	☐	☐
	☐	☐	☐
	☐	☐	☐
	☐	☐	☐
5	☐	☐	☐
	☐	☐	☐
	☐	☐	☐
	☐	☐	☐
	☐	☐	☐
	☐	☐	☐
6	☐	☐	☐
	☐	☐	☐
	☐	☐	☐
	☐	☐	☐
	☐	☐	☐
	☐	☐	☐

WEEK:

★ As students get older, consider setting aside monthly conference times when you can regularly check in with each other about how learning is going and make any adjustments that could improve your daily routine. Remember: Your plan doesn't have to be set in stone.

THURSDAY	FRIDAY	SAT / SUN
☐	☐	☐
☐	☐	☐
☐	☐	☐
☐	☐	☐
☐	☐	☐
☐	☐	☐
☐	☐	☐
☐	☐	☐
☐	☐	☐
☐	☐	☐
☐	☐	☐
☐	☐	☐
☐	☐	☐
☐	☐	☐
☐	☐	☐
☐	☐	☐
☐	☐	☐
☐	☐	☐
☐	☐	☐
☐	☐	☐
☐	☐	☐
☐	☐	☐
☐	☐	☐
☐	☐	☐
☐	☐	☐
☐	☐	☐
☐	☐	☐
☐	☐	☐
☐	☐	☐
☐	☐	☐
☐	☐	☐
☐	☐	☐
☐	☐	☐
☐	☐	☐
☐	☐	☐
☐	☐	☐

WEEK:

Extras

1

2

3

4

5

6

EXTRAS

Grades

We have to be continually jumping off cliffs and developing our wings on the way down. —KURT VONNEGUT

	SUBJECT	GRADE
1		
2		
3		
4		
5		
6		

GRADES

WEEK

	MONDAY	TUESDAY	WEDNESDAY
1			
2			
3			
4			
5			
6			

WEEK:

I imagine good teaching as a circle of earnest people sitting down to ask each other meaningful questions. I don't see it as a handing down of answers. —ALICE WALKER

THURSDAY	FRIDAY	SAT / SUN
☐	☐	☐
☐	☐	☐
☐	☐	☐
☐	☐	☐
☐	☐	☐
☐	☐	☐
☐	☐	☐
☐	☐	☐
☐	☐	☐
☐	☐	☐
☐	☐	☐
☐	☐	☐
☐	☐	☐
☐	☐	☐
☐	☐	☐
☐	☐	☐
☐	☐	☐
☐	☐	☐
☐	☐	☐
☐	☐	☐
☐	☐	☐
☐	☐	☐
☐	☐	☐
☐	☐	☐
☐	☐	☐
☐	☐	☐
☐	☐	☐
☐	☐	☐
☐	☐	☐
☐	☐	☐
☐	☐	☐
☐	☐	☐
☐	☐	☐
☐	☐	☐
☐	☐	☐
☐	☐	☐

WEEK:

Extras

1

2

3

4

5

6

EXTRAS

Grades

It had long since come to my attention that people of accomplishment rarely sat back and let things happen to them. They went out and happened to things.
—LEONARDO DAVINCI

	SUBJECT	GRADE
1		
2		
3		
4		
5		
6		

WEEK

	MONDAY	TUESDAY	WEDNESDAY
1			
2			
3			
4			
5			
6			

WEEK:

Few things help an individual more than to place responsibility upon him and let him know you trust him. —BOOKER T. WASHINGTON

THURSDAY	FRIDAY	SAT / SUN
☐	☐	☐
☐	☐	☐
☐	☐	☐
☐	☐	☐
☐	☐	☐
☐	☐	☐
☐	☐	☐
☐	☐	☐
☐	☐	☐
☐	☐	☐
☐	☐	☐
☐	☐	☐
☐	☐	☐
☐	☐	☐
☐	☐	☐
☐	☐	☐
☐	☐	☐
☐	☐	☐
☐	☐	☐
☐	☐	☐
☐	☐	☐
☐	☐	☐
☐	☐	☐
☐	☐	☐
☐	☐	☐
☐	☐	☐
☐	☐	☐
☐	☐	☐
☐	☐	☐
☐	☐	☐
☐	☐	☐
☐	☐	☐
☐	☐	☐
☐	☐	☐
☐	☐	☐
☐	☐	☐

Extras

1

2

3

4

5

6

EXTRAS

Grades

I get up every morning both wanting to change the world and to have one heck of a good time. Sometimes this makes planning the day difficult. —E.B. WHITE

	SUBJECT	GRADE
1		
2		
3		
4		
5		
6		

GRADES

WEEK

	MONDAY	TUESDAY	WEDNESDAY
1	☐	☐	☐
	☐	☐	☐
	☐	☐	☐
	☐	☐	☐
	☐	☐	☐
	☐	☐	☐
2	☐	☐	☐
	☐	☐	☐
	☐	☐	☐
	☐	☐	☐
	☐	☐	☐
	☐	☐	☐
3	☐	☐	☐
	☐	☐	☐
	☐	☐	☐
	☐	☐	☐
	☐	☐	☐
	☐	☐	☐
4	☐	☐	☐
	☐	☐	☐
	☐	☐	☐
	☐	☐	☐
	☐	☐	☐
	☐	☐	☐
5	☐	☐	☐
	☐	☐	☐
	☐	☐	☐
	☐	☐	☐
	☐	☐	☐
	☐	☐	☐
6	☐	☐	☐
	☐	☐	☐
	☐	☐	☐
	☐	☐	☐
	☐	☐	☐
	☐	☐	☐

Knowledge emerges only through invention and reinvention, through the restless, impatient, continuing, hopeful inquiry human beings pursue in the world, with the world, and with each other. —PAULO FREIRE

THURSDAY	FRIDAY	SAT / SUN
☐	☐	☐
☐	☐	☐
☐	☐	☐
☐	☐	☐
☐	☐	☐
☐	☐	☐
☐	☐	☐
☐	☐	☐
☐	☐	☐
☐	☐	☐
☐	☐	☐
☐	☐	☐
☐	☐	☐
☐	☐	☐
☐	☐	☐
☐	☐	☐
☐	☐	☐
☐	☐	☐
☐	☐	☐
☐	☐	☐
☐	☐	☐
☐	☐	☐
☐	☐	☐
☐	☐	☐
☐	☐	☐
☐	☐	☐
☐	☐	☐
☐	☐	☐
☐	☐	☐
☐	☐	☐
☐	☐	☐
☐	☐	☐
☐	☐	☐
☐	☐	☐
☐	☐	☐
☐	☐	☐

Extras

1

2

3

4

5

6

EXTRAS

Grades

It's much easier, after all, to learn mathematics from someone who's made a few mistakes. It's impossible to learn it from someone who always gets it right. —JOHN C. LENNOX

	SUBJECT	GRADE
1		
2		
3		
4		
5		
6		

GRADES

WEEK

WEEK:

	MONDAY	TUESDAY	WEDNESDAY
1			
2			
3			
4			
5			
6			

Education is learning what you didn't even know you didn't know.
—DANIEL J. BOORSTIN

THURSDAY	FRIDAY	SAT / SUN
☐	☐	☐
☐	☐	☐
☐	☐	☐
☐	☐	☐
☐	☐	☐
☐	☐	☐
☐	☐	☐
☐	☐	☐
☐	☐	☐
☐	☐	☐
☐	☐	☐
☐	☐	☐
☐	☐	☐
☐	☐	☐
☐	☐	☐
☐	☐	☐
☐	☐	☐
☐	☐	☐
☐	☐	☐
☐	☐	☐
☐	☐	☐
☐	☐	☐
☐	☐	☐
☐	☐	☐
☐	☐	☐
☐	☐	☐
☐	☐	☐
☐	☐	☐
☐	☐	☐
☐	☐	☐
☐	☐	☐
☐	☐	☐
☐	☐	☐
☐	☐	☐
☐	☐	☐
☐	☐	☐

WEEK:

Extras

1

2

3

4

5

6

EXTRAS

Grades

That is what learning is. You suddenly understand something you've understood all your life, but in a new way. —DORIS LESSING

	SUBJECT	GRADE
1		
2		
3		
4		
5		
6		

GRADES

WEEK

	MONDAY	TUESDAY	WEDNESDAY
1	☐	☐	☐
	☐	☐	☐
	☐	☐	☐
	☐	☐	☐
	☐	☐	☐
	☐	☐	☐
2	☐	☐	☐
	☐	☐	☐
	☐	☐	☐
	☐	☐	☐
	☐	☐	☐
	☐	☐	☐
3	☐	☐	☐
	☐	☐	☐
	☐	☐	☐
	☐	☐	☐
	☐	☐	☐
	☐	☐	☐
4	☐	☐	☐
	☐	☐	☐
	☐	☐	☐
	☐	☐	☐
	☐	☐	☐
	☐	☐	☐
5	☐	☐	☐
	☐	☐	☐
	☐	☐	☐
	☐	☐	☐
	☐	☐	☐
	☐	☐	☐
6	☐	☐	☐
	☐	☐	☐
	☐	☐	☐
	☐	☐	☐
	☐	☐	☐
	☐	☐	☐

In the end, the secret to learning is so simple: Forget about it. Think only about whatever you love. Follow it, do it, dream about it. One day, you will glance up at your collection of Japanese literature, or trip over the solar oven you built, and it will hit you: learning was there all the time, happening by itself. —GRACE LLEWELLYN

THURSDAY	FRIDAY	SAT / SUN
☐	☐	☐
☐	☐	☐
☐	☐	☐
☐	☐	☐
☐	☐	☐
☐	☐	☐
☐	☐	☐
☐	☐	☐
☐	☐	☐
☐	☐	☐
☐	☐	☐
☐	☐	☐
☐	☐	☐
☐	☐	☐
☐	☐	☐
☐	☐	☐
☐	☐	☐
☐	☐	☐
☐	☐	☐
☐	☐	☐
☐	☐	☐
☐	☐	☐
☐	☐	☐
☐	☐	☐
☐	☐	☐
☐	☐	☐
☐	☐	☐
☐	☐	☐
☐	☐	☐
☐	☐	☐
☐	☐	☐
☐	☐	☐
☐	☐	☐
☐	☐	☐
☐	☐	☐
☐	☐	☐

WEEK:

Extras

1

2

3

4

5

6

EXTRAS

Grades

Let us remember: one book, one pen, one child, and one teacher can change the world. —MALALA YOUSAFZAI

	SUBJECT	GRADE
1		
2		
3		
4		
5		
6		

GRADES

WEEK

	MONDAY	TUESDAY	WEDNESDAY
1	☐ ☐ ☐ ☐ ☐ ☐	☐ ☐ ☐ ☐ ☐ ☐	☐ ☐ ☐ ☐ ☐ ☐
2	☐ ☐ ☐ ☐ ☐ ☐	☐ ☐ ☐ ☐ ☐ ☐	☐ ☐ ☐ ☐ ☐ ☐
3	☐ ☐ ☐ ☐ ☐ ☐	☐ ☐ ☐ ☐ ☐ ☐	☐ ☐ ☐ ☐ ☐ ☐
4	☐ ☐ ☐ ☐ ☐ ☐	☐ ☐ ☐ ☐ ☐ ☐	☐ ☐ ☐ ☐ ☐ ☐
5	☐ ☐ ☐ ☐ ☐ ☐	☐ ☐ ☐ ☐ ☐ ☐	☐ ☐ ☐ ☐ ☐ ☐
6	☐ ☐ ☐ ☐ ☐ ☐	☐ ☐ ☐ ☐ ☐ ☐	☐ ☐ ☐ ☐ ☐ ☐

Would you like me to give you a formula for success? It's quite simple, really: Double your rate of failure. You are thinking of failure as the enemy of success. But it isn't at all. You can be discouraged by failure or you can learn from it, so go ahead and make mistakes. Make all you can. Because remember that's where you will find success. —THOMAS J. WATSON

THURSDAY	FRIDAY	SAT / SUN
☐	☐	☐
☐	☐	☐
☐	☐	☐
☐	☐	☐
☐	☐	☐
☐	☐	☐
☐	☐	☐
☐	☐	☐
☐	☐	☐
☐	☐	☐
☐	☐	☐
☐	☐	☐
☐	☐	☐
☐	☐	☐
☐	☐	☐
☐	☐	☐
☐	☐	☐
☐	☐	☐
☐	☐	☐
☐	☐	☐
☐	☐	☐
☐	☐	☐
☐	☐	☐
☐	☐	☐
☐	☐	☐
☐	☐	☐
☐	☐	☐
☐	☐	☐
☐	☐	☐
☐	☐	☐
☐	☐	☐
☐	☐	☐
☐	☐	☐
☐	☐	☐
☐	☐	☐
☐	☐	☐

Extras

1

2

3

4

5

6

EXTRAS

Grades

If you want your children to turn out well, spend twice as much time with them, and half as much money. —ABIGAIL VAN BUREN

	SUBJECT	GRADE
1		
2		
3		
4		
5		
6		

GRADES

The Year in Review ____________

YEAR

YEAR:

1

2

3

MY YEAR IN REVIEW

Education is not to reform students or amuse them or to make them expert technicians. It is to unsettle their minds, widen their horizons, inflame their intellects, teach them to think straight, if possible. —ROBERT M. HUTCHINS

4

5

6

YEAR:

Notes

Resources

Whether you are a brand new homeschool parent or an experienced homeschooler, these resources are great sources of inspiration and practical advice.

ORGANIZATIONS

SEA Homeschoolers

seahomeschoolers.com

Secular Eclectic Academic (SEA) Homeschoolers is an active community of secular homeschoolers with an information-rich website, supportive Facebook groups for every homeschool stage and interest, and a national homeschool conference.

BOOKS

Bauer, Susan Wise and Jessie Wise. *The Well-Trained Mind: A Guide to Classical Education at Home*. New York: W.W. Norton & Company, 2016.

This is the fourth edition of the book that launched the classical homeschooling movement when it was published in 1999.

Hirsch, E.D., Jr., and John Holden. *Books to Build On: A Grade-by-Grade Resource Guide for Parents and Teachers*. Crystal Lake, IL: Delta Publishing Company, 1996.

If your homeschool is books-based, this will quickly become your essential reading list.

Holt, John. *How Children Learn*. New York: Da Capo Press, 1995.

Holt's work inspired early homeschoolers with its child-led, interest-driven philosophy, and contemporary homeschoolers can find reassurance and inspiration in its pages, too.

Khan, Salman. *The One World Schoolhouse: Education Reimagined*. New York: Twelve, 2013.

The founder of Khan Academy considers the future of education.

Rupp, Rebecca. *Home Learning Year by Year: How to Design a Homeschool Curriculum from Preschool Through High School*. New York: Three Rivers Press, 2000.

For everyone who wonders *"What should we be learning in this grade?"* or *"What do we do all day?"* this book has practical answers.

Weldon, Laura Grace. *Free Range Learning: How Homeschooling Changes Everything*. Chino Valley, AZ: Hohm Press, 2010.

Its emphasis is on unschooling, but all kinds of homeschoolers can appreciate this book's homeschooling-as-a-lifestyle philosophy and tips for making learning part of everyday life.

WEBSITES

Homeschool Buyers Co-Op

https://www.homeschoolbuyersco-op.org/

Take advantage of group discounts on popular curriculum through this online co-op.

SECULAR HOMESCHOOL FORUMS

http://www.secularhomeschool.com/forum.php

Conversation about secular homeschool materials, resources, and methods.

home/school/life

http://homeschoollifemag.com/
Publishes a weekly blog, quarterly magazine, and occasional podcast for secular homeschoolers.

Acknowledgments

I never stop appreciating how lucky I am to get to write about homeschooling for a living, and I'm so thankful to all the people who helped make this book a reality. Thank you so much:

To my editor Susan Randol, whose intelligent criticism and thoughtful review made working on this book a pleasure.

To Marthine Satris, who was nice enough to think I might do a good job on this project.

To Meg Woodcheke, who did an absolutely beautiful job bringing this planner to life—this book is really her baby as much as mine.

To the amazing team at Callisto, including Andrew Yackira, Kim Ciabattari, Myryah Irby, Michael Counter Jr., Ashley Casteel, and Nancy Freeborn. You guys make it look easy.

To all the wonderful people at *home/school/life* magazine, especially editors Shelli Bond Pabis and Suzanne Rezelman and our writers, including Beverly Burgess, Amy Hood, Maggie Martin, Carrie Pomeroy, and Patricia Zaballos. I've learned so much from all of you about homeschooling, parenting, and life over the years.

Always, especially to Jason. To Shelly. And to Olwen and Thor, who have been the nicest of all possible guinea pigs on our family's homeschool adventure. I love you guys!

About the Author

AMY SHARONY is the founder and editor of *home/school/life* magazine, a quarterly magazine for secular homeschoolers. She lives in Atlanta with her husband, her two happily homeschooled children, and one very spoiled dog.